PARTY games

Manageable parties for twos to tens

Nicola Adamson

Illustrated by

Jan Lewis

Macdonald

Author's acknowledgements

I would like to express my thanks to Stephanie Warren for sharing her cake-making expertise, and to Christine Rudnicki for her ideas, to Sandra Wake, Terry Porter and Coco for inviting me to some excellent children's parties, to Katie Abbot, Laura Clarke, Amy Cornwell, Charis and Quentin Croft, Ruth Dallot, Louisa Lamptey, Daniel, Zella and Ben Page, Tristan Porter, Jesse Reiss, and Matthew Warren for enthusiastic games playing and partying, to Anne Yelland for making sense of my text, to my husband Stephen for his confidence and support, and especially to my children, Sam, Daisy, George and Alice, for giving me literally years of party-giving experience.

The photograph on p.13 was supplied by Pictor International.

Conceived and produced by
Swallow Books
260 Pentonville Road
London N1 9JY

Editor: Anne Yelland
Art director: Elaine Partington
Designers: Stephen Bitti and Jacqueline Palmer
Illustrator: Jan Lewis
Photography: Tony Timmington
Studio: Del and Co

Copyright © Swallow Publishing Ltd 1989

First published in Great Britain in 1989
by Macdonald & Co (Publishers) Ltd
Headway House
66–73 Shoe Lane
London EC4P 4AB

A member of Maxwell Pergamon
Publishing Corporation plc

British Library Cataloguing in Publication Data

Adamson, Nicola
    Party games: manageable parties for twos to tens.
    1. Entertainments: children's parties – Manuals
    I. Title
    793.2'1

    ISBN 0–356–16811–5
    ISBN 0–356–16681–3 Pbk

Typeset by Opus, Oxford
Colour origination and printing by Imago Publishing Ltd

Contents

Introduction

Children's parties are supposed to be fun. This may seem a rather obvious statement with which to start a book about party games, but it's amazing how many parents view the prospect with dread, whatever the age of the children in question. If they're two, there are bound to be tantrums, they say, and if they're ten, they're bound to be tearaways. Yet people go on giving parties, year after year, for their offspring, gritting their teeth and just counting the minutes until the little monsters have all gone home again. It needn't be like that, of course, and nine times out of ten it isn't. Nevertheless, it's quite natural to view an influx of ten or more children into your home with apprehension, especially if you don't know them all very well.

Party Games aims to help you get over that apprehension and approach the occasion as something to be enjoyed by all – adults as well as children. Surprisingly, it isn't only parents who find children's parties a bit of a trial – lots of children find them difficult too, both as hosts and as guests.

Planning is the key to a successful party, but paradoxically, so is flexibility. The children have come expecting to have a good time — and the older they are, the better they are at making their own entertainment. Providing a structure is all that you need to do. That structure should include lots of varied games and activities, something delicious and substantial to eat, and a few prizes and gifts to add an element of surprise to the proceedings. In these pages you'll find advice on planning and timing the party, preparing the food, and tips to make things to go with a swing. Then there are more than 120 games for all ages and occasions, to be played indoors and out. The age range is two years to ten, and the suitability of the games is indicated according to age group in each case. Remember, though, that sometimes a little variation is all that is necessary to make a simple game sophisticated enough for the most streetwise of ten-year-olds. So, with a little help from your friends and a lot of goodwill from your guests, get partying!

Planning a party

The key to giving a successful children's party is planning – it reduces chaos, disappointment and adult frustration. Unless you're inviting four friends round for an impromptu tea (and why not?), you really need to think about a party at least a month ahead, three months if you want to book a good children's entertainer in a busy holiday period like Christmas or Easter.

The occasion

There are any number of reasons for giving a party, although birthdays are the most popular and the most universal. Celebrating someone's birthday is always something worth doing – it often starts with half a dozen mums with their one-year-olds crawling around on a rug and throwing cake at the cat. But birthday parties involving organized games and activities can't really start until children reach the age of two, and even then they need an awful lot of adult assistance.

There is something comfortably familiar about a birthday party – children enjoy the ordered predictability of giving presents, playing games, tea, the cake, the candles, singing 'Happy Birthday', and so on. You'll be surprised at the extent to which even ten-year-olds respond to this formula, even if part of it does take place after the football game or in the swimming-pool café.

Birthdays of course aren't the only reason for giving parties, and if you would rather have one that didn't involve gifts, or if you are away for your child's birthday or simply want to do something different, there are always the major religious festivals to celebrate (Christmas, Easter, Jewish or Chinese New Year, Diwali, and so on), or Hallowe'en, Guy Fawkes Night, May Day, Midsummer's Eve – all of which present themselves as occasions for a theme party – or perhaps you want to have a class reunion, or a farewell for someone moving away, or congratulations for passing an exam.

It's a good idea to bring a small element of the actual festival being celebrated into a party at , say, Christmas or Easter. Have carols by candlelight in the garden, or turn *Follow the Trail* or *Treasure Hunt* into an Easter-egg hunt (see pp.112 and 114).

If you have fireworks or a bonfire or barbecue (in fact anything involving a naked flame) at home, make sure you have plenty of other adults on hand to supervise. Fireworks must be kept in a closed metal container, and as you're taking responsibility for other people's children for the duration of the party, don't let any of them touch the fireworks or bonfire – with no exceptions, your own child included. Children get very excited on these occasions, especially in a group, and do silly things which they know are stupid, even dangerous, and which they would never do individually. Forestall the possibility of trouble by simply not letting any of them anywhere near!

It's exciting for a group of nine- to ten-year-olds (with their parents' express permission) to have a midnight feast on Midsummer's Eve. (Strictly speaking this is 21/22 June, but you could cheat if that's not a convenient time!) Unless parents come too or are prepared to turn out to collect them, make this a small group, start at nine and finish at midnight, then let them all stay the night, camping out in the garden if that's suitable (or in one bedroom). You could do this on New Year's Eve too, especially if you know their parents well – it could be a really happy occasion for all, with no worries about babysitting.

Blowing out the candles on the cake is the high point of any birthday party.

9

An energetic game of Oranges and Lemons *is perfect for a summer party in the garden.*

The place

The space available often dictates the type of party you give. Once you have decided to have a party, look at the space available at home and think about what you can and can't do there. If your child is six or older, bring him or her into the consultation. It is very important to involve them right from the start to avoid too much over-vivid fantasizing about the event. Children set enormous store by parties and anticipate the event with great excitement, so that even the most extrovert four-year-old can be overcome by tears or shyness on the day, and imaginative seven- to ten-year-olds have been

known to seem positively ungrateful when the reality doesn't quite live up to the picture they have built up inside their heads. It is probably best to give under-sixes as little warning as possible – be matter-of-fact about the preparations and on the day try to have them taken out or distracted in some way before the party.

A children's party needs a minimum of two spaces – one for the meal and one for the games – so if you don't feel able to give over your living-room to fifteen six-year-olds playing *Musical Bumps*, or (more particularly) twenty ten-year-olds

10

having a disco, then find somewhere else to take them. You do need to be able to clear a fairly large area for games, since you have to allow some of them to be quite energetic or you will find chaos reigns during the meal. A floor space of about 3m × 3m (12ft × 12ft) is just about big enough as long as there is no furniture in the space at all. And you must be able to have the food elsewhere; you need someone to help get it ready and it must not be in sight at the beginning of the party or your efforts to involve the children in the games will be useless. Party food is too distracting!

If you're not going to have dancing, older children don't need quite so much 'open' space, because you can involve them in more sophisticated pen-and-paper games like *What's on the Tray?* or *Consequences* (see pp.67 and 71), or in whole house games like *Hide and Seek*, *Sardines* or even *Murder* (see pp.82 and 110). It is important, however, to mark off any parts of the house which are strictly out of bounds (lock the doors for safety) and shut out pets who may be frightened by a large number of unknown children. Otherwise perfectly placid dogs have been known to nip inquisitive children who disturb them while they're hiding under the bed!

Don't rule out parties in flats but check that the people around you know what is happening – especially those downstairs! In fact a purpose-built flat in a block may offer useful extras – like long corridors for *Barmy Bowling* (see p.79, but check the neighbours, and the caretaker, don't mind), or a relatively spacious central lobby inside the flat where you could set up a game of *Silly Squash* (see p.86). But another safety point – if you're higher than ground floor and you've a balcony and/or fire escape access, keep the doors locked and out of bounds, for obvious reasons.

For fine weather parties, gardens are a boon, and even a small backyard is worth utilizing for the younger age groups. They (and you) seem to feel more at ease in the open air. Small gardens are no good for the sort of action games and races recommended for older children, especially anything involving running or cycling – let alone football or frisbee – so that's the time to go to the nearest park. It needn't actually *be* the nearest if you've got plenty of willing adults to help ferry; if you think a park or open space a bit further afield is better or more attractive or simply would make a change, suggest a particular rendezvous and take a picnic. Otherwise, it's all back home for the meal.

HIRING A HALL

If your own home is not big enough or you really don't want two dozen ten-year-olds rampaging round and dropping cola on the carpet, think about hiring somewhere else to hold the party. Community or church halls are a good bet, and local leisure or sports centres often have a room which is rented for functions. Costs vary – your local church or playgroup hall is probably a lot cheaper than the sports centre. If you can manage to hire a really good-sized space, or one which has access to the outside, you might be able to hire inflatables for the children to play on. These are so popular that you hardly need to organize games at all (except possibly quiet ones at the end when they are all exhausted). Inflatables need close supervision; children can get wild and jump on each other, so limit the number at any one time, make sure they take their shoes, socks and any jewellery or watches off, and don't let them jump near the edge or off the edge because they can easily misjudge the force of their bouncing and land awkwardly.

If you're friendly with a local farmer, you may be able to borrow a barn – why not have a real barn dance? Equally, don't be afraid to ask a close friend with a bigger house or garden if you could hold your party at their place. If they have children of their own they will understand your problems, and if you make sure that they don't have to do anything, especially with clearing up afterwards, that you provide all the crockery and cutlery (a good case for disposables, see p.20), that they are not going to be out of pocket at all (offer to pay for electricity or gas used, and for all telephone calls), and their children can join in as well, this could be a good arrangement. Clinch it by offering your services when it's your friend's turn to play host.

PARTIES OUT

You don't, of course, have to give a conventional party at all. (In fact many parents give up parties at home after the age of seven until the children are old enough to organize them for themselves!) Many leisure pools now hire out their teaching pools to private parties, and often will provide a birthday tea in the café or canteen afterwards. With inflatables and floats, this can be an enjoyable occasion for small children. Though most public pools do have lifeguards on duty, make sure that you have as many adults present as possible to help non-swimmers and to stop silliness and splashing from any others. You also need to keep an eye open in case one of the more inquisitive children decides to wander off to the main pool.

Older children may enjoy going to the cinema, a show, the zoo, the fair (line up extra supervisory help for the two latter options), the bowling alley, the sports centre or to watch their favourite sport. If you and your child decide that this is better than a conventional party, limit it to eight children (including your own), especially if you're going to take them on public transport. If you have or can borrow or rent a campervan or minibus, then this might be preferable. The games on pp.116–9 will help to while away the journey.

Cinemas, theatres and sports are all popular but you could try something a bit more unconventional. If you're going to the ballet or theatre, why not ask if it's possible to go backstage? Many companies, especially if they are public-funded, have education departments so this won't seem an outlandish request, and they may well respond favourably, even for a small group. Take the children to a modern art gallery (and get them to do a version of something they saw when they get home, with

Taking a group of children out to the swimming pool is a fun alternative to a conventional party.

prizes for the best pastiche); they go to museums on school trips, but there may well be something a bit unusual tucked away in or near your neighbourhood – a restored, working flour mill, for instance, a collection of rare farm breeds, an otter sanctuary or a butterfly park. Ask at your local library or Tourist Information Centre and see if they can recommend something that you and your child hadn't thought of.

You could organize a tour of the local fire station or police station; or of a pottery or similar craft workshop; or even of a chocolate factory! Public relations departments love to service unusual requests as it reflects well on the company image.

All these will need plenty of advance warning to arrange something – you may well have to get special permission first and then make your arrangements round their date, rather than the other way round. Many places that charge entry fees do make reductions for groups. Although the minimum number is often as many as twenty people, it is always worth asking, especially if you explain the nature of the occasion.

13

Paying for help

You may feel that you can't manage a party on your own and that you are prepared to pay someone else to take some or all the responsibility off your shoulders. Hiring an entertainer is one way to relieve some of the burden and keep the children occupied for at least half an hour. Good entertainers, however, can be quite expensive, and if they *are* good they will be booked up, at weekends especially, for months ahead. This is where forethought is vital. Finding a good entertainer is a bit hit and miss – word of mouth recommendation is always best. Note down the names of any entertainers that you like who you see at another child's party; ask your friends for recommendations and also ask at your child's school (they sometimes get entertainers in for end-of-term treats and such like). Specialist children's theatre companies and local arts centres could also be a useful source of information.

Talk to the entertainer beforehand and before committing yourself; make sure you know exactly what it is going to cost (including extras like VAT or travel expenses), what facilities he or she is going to need, and how long he or she needs to set up any equipment. You have to be able to let an entertainer set up privately – seeing the puppet theatre go up or the white rabbit being hidden in the hat rather takes the surprise out of the occasion! If you haven't got enough rooms, make sure the entertainer sets up while the children are eating. Some younger children are irrationally frightened by clowns, puppets or things that go bang. Go through the routine verbally with the entertainer beforehand so you know what to expect and when to field the nervous children. Always have somewhere else for them to go and play quietly while the entertainer is performing (see p.40); you should never force a child to watch or to participate against his or her will – there could well be a scene which will spoil it for all the others and you might in any case reinforce whatever difficulty the child is experiencing.

On the other side of the coin, make sure you establish with the performer the age and sophistication of the group that he or she will be entertaining. It is disappointing for everyone if the tricks are so simple, for instance, that a seven-year-old can announce 'I know how you do that, it's in my book of conjuring tricks.' If there are one or two older ones in a group of young children, have the entertainer gear it to the younger age group, but take the older ones aside and make sure they don't interrupt. Clowns, comics, conjurers, singers and puppet shows are perennial favourites – don't try to be too original in your choice because you're all more likely to be disappointed.

MOBILE DISCOS AND OTHER MUSIC

If you're giving a party for a large group of nine- and ten-year-olds (and maybe older), think about hiring a mobile disco. These usually come complete with DJ, who will be able to act as master of ceremonies and games leader as well in some cases. Mobile discos usually advertise in the *Yellow Pages* and local papers. Ring round and get quotes and talk to the DJ to make sure he or she understands the age group to be entertained so that the record selection can be geared to the right level. Before you commit yourself to any particular outfit, make sure you know exactly what they need in terms of space and power supply; you don't want to be presented with an enormous bill for extras which you weren't budgeting for.

You could, of course, hire the equipment and act as DJ yourself, or simply use your own sound system. Use a powerful flashlight for the spotlight dance: as the children dance, swing the light around and focus on one particular child, stop the music and then get them to do a forfeit. Choose something silly, like singing a verse of a song, standing on their hands, whistling 'Colonel Bogey' or similar, reciting a simple tongue-twister twenty times, drinking a glass of water backwards, and so on. Get your own child to think up suitable horrors!

Younger children don't need the expense of a complete disco, but will enjoy music. See if you can find someone who can play the piano or the guitar and sing. Children respond particularly well to live music, and it is easier to gear the music to their preferences. You may even have a talented friend or relation who could be persuaded to come along and play just for the fun of it. Hiring a group to play for older children, however, is risky – the group's repertoire may well be limited so it's best to play safe with music supplied electronically.

HANDING IT OVER TO SOMEONE ELSE

There are companies and individuals who, for a fee, will take over the organization and running of your party completely for you. This can be a boon for working parents, or anyone who just wants to join in without any worry. Once again, personal recommendation, the local paper or *Yellow Pages* will help you here. Some of these services are very sophisticated – they'll do the food, provide entertainment, even hire a hall for you – but this, of course, is all reflected in the price. Companies like this are springing up all the time, especially in big cities, but you can find less expensive outfits almost anywhere, and they can be very good value. Enterprising teenagers have been known to set themselves up as party planners as a sort of side-line – ask your friends, or even suggest it to reliable kids who want to earn pocket money. It will at least take some of the effort off your shoulders. The bigger firms often offer a choice of service – they will provide puppet shows, clowns, or a disco for an hour or so, say, or take over the whole party. You really can pick and choose now in what is obviously a growth area.

Party themes

Lots of people like to vary the interest of their children's parties by suggesting a theme. There is not much point in providing an elaborate theme for children under five – the only people who are going to appreciate the effort are the other adults. There's nothing wrong with that, of course, but children's parties are really for the children to enjoy first and foremost. You could save yourself a lot of effort which could more usefully be put into doing things that pre-school children do enjoy, namely lots of singing and dancing games. You could, however, try an easy theme which would be appreciated by the under-fives, like zoo animals, the farm, the circus or a teddy bears' picnic. This is particularly good – indoors or out – since all you have to do is ask everyone to bring a teddy with them. You could decorate the rooms with cut-out teddies, have a teddy bear's picnic cake, make as many items of food as possible into teddy bear shapes, play teddy bear *Pairs* (see p.115) and lay places at table for the teddies as well as the guests. It shouldn't be too difficult to find disposable plates and cups with teddy bear motifs and even teddy-shaped balloons. This same idea can be applied successfully to the other under-fives themes. If you're going to hire an entertainer, make sure he or she knows what the theme is too.

Theme parties are much appreciated by the over-fives and they're a good way to persuade super-cool sub-teens that a party is a good idea *without* a disco. They also have definite advantages over fancy dress parties. If you have neither the time nor the skill to make a fancy dress costume, and you can't or don't want to go to the expense of hiring one, fancy dress parties are a nightmare. It's also very hard to be original at an open-style fancy dress party – there's a stage when all the little girls come as fairies or ballerinas, and the boys as policemen or masters of the universe. In fact a lot of children are resistant to fancy dress – a theme party is a much better idea.

Themes can become increasingly sophisticated depending on the age of the children. Some random ideas are the Wild West, Oriental, Olympic sports, movie stars, magic, space, the sea, or types of work. These all allow for plenty of scope and the widest possible interpretation. If your theme is going to call for a certain amount of dressing up, make sure that it is clear that the children have to make their own costumes. This gets round the basic problem of fancy dress for the less-well-off and non-crafty families, and you can give prizes for the best and most original interpretations of the theme, as well as the best-made costume.

Older children enjoy the challenge of a colour theme party – where balloons, clothes, furnishings, even face paints, can be colour co-ordinated.

One of the simplest and most effective themes is to designate a colour scheme for the party. Make everything purple, or red, or black and white, or silver, for instance, and design everything from invitations to icing on the cake in the party colour scheme. Get your children to help with the decorations – a purple party could have purple streamers everywhere, and you could dye some old sheets and use them as purple wall hangings. Provide purple face paints for those who hadn't thought of it, and colour as much food as you can with blackcurrant cordial. It's lurid, but great fun and children enter into it with gusto, coming up with some surprising ideas themselves.

If you're going for an Olympic theme, why not have an odd-ball Olympic competition too? You could organize silly sports based on some of the games given on pp.88–91 and 96–9, and provide Olympic medals as prizes. Vary things a bit by awarding medals to the last three or the three who are placed exactly in the middle. If you do this completely randomly it gives everyone a chance to win something and adds an element of unpredictability to the proceedings.

The timetable

Planning a party really is a question of having a week by week (at some times of the year, even longer than this), day by day, then hour by hour schedule of events so that you know nothing has been forgotten. If you make a proper plan and stick to it, ticking off events as they happen, you will avoid any last-minute panics and feel confident that all will go well.

Forward planning

Forward planning is vital in giving a successful and happy children's party. You really have to think ahead by as much as three months if you want to book a popular entertainer during a traditional holiday period; at other times, a month ahead is usually enough for the average children's party. This isn't meant to be off-putting, it's just that children tend to lead very busy social lives, and if you decide to give a party you need to sit down and work out with your child the best day to have it. For instance, if the party is to celebrate your child's eighth birthday on a Tuesday during term time, would it be better to have the party after school on the day, or at the weekend before or after the actual day? What after-school or weekend commitments have to be accommodated?

Once you have sorted out these problems together, you need to decide what kind of party you are going to have and where. If you're having it at home then you can arrange it to suit you, but if you're hiring a hall or going to a show then obviously it depends on when the hall is available, or what time the matinee performance starts and finishes. If you want to hire an entertainer or a mobile disco, when can they be fitted in? Do you want them there for the whole party or only for an hour or so?

The next step is the invitations. Draw up a guest list with your child and be realistic about the numbers you are prepared to cater for. In fact, catering is literally the easiest thing to plan – it's whether you think you can cope with the numbers when they're not actually eating that should exercise you! If you think you can manage a dozen or more, that's fine, but it still means he or she can't ask the whole class *and* the favourite cousins *and*

the children you met on the beach on your last summer holiday! Try to persuade your child to invite a good mix; although you may feel worried about hurting someone's feelings it is still probably better in the long run not to invite one outsider among a group of children who know each other very well, unless you know he or she is very outgoing.

If you decide on a theme party set the scene right from the start with your invitations. Get your child to draw a suitable picture and have it photocopied several times, or buy blank cards and make each one individual. If you show that you're going to make something of the theme without being too serious about it, then the guests will be more likely to enter into the spirit of it.

Send out the invitations about three weeks ahead, once you have all the advance details finalized. And make it clear you really do want an RSVP – provide a tear-off slip to be filled in – and always put your phone number as well as address on the invitation. Pin the guest list up somewhere prominent and tick off the acceptances when you hear them directly – not secondhand from someone down the road who thinks Johnny's coming because he heard his sister talking about it in the playground! If you haven't heard from everybody a week before the party, ring round and find out for yourself. This isn't being pushy, it's being practical, especially if you're paying for catering or a hall or buying tickets.

Jessica is having a fancy hat party

on 15
4.00p

RSVP
Tel 60

You are invited to Emma's birthday barbecue on 4th June at 4.00 pm

RSVP
27 Azalea Avenue
Tel 372914

Please come to Tom's monster party on 22 January at 3.00pm

RSVP 103 St John's Road
Tel 906732

irthday
October

eet

Another thing to check when you're getting the replies in is how many adults are going to be around too. For a younger children's party, up to five and beyond in some cases, there are always going to be a certain number of adults accompanying their children for different reasons. Some young children are nervous and don't want to be left; some may have come from outside your immediate neighbourhood and it would be impractical for their parents to go away and come back again two hours later if they live anything from twenty minutes' journey upwards away. It's quite good to have a few extra adults – no-one minds being asked to give a hand, even if it's only to encourage their own child to join in the games. If you're having a more elaborate party for older children, especially one that involves any kind of foray into the outside world, you will need help, and if you're planning competitive games, then you'll need 'umpires'. Always have someone in the kitchen to help put the meal on the table and make drinks for adults while you get on with the serious business of playing games. Grandparents usually enjoy coming to children's parties and are often happy to take on this back-seat role; otherwise ask a close friend with whom you will be able to swap places when his or her turn comes to give a party.

Some people ask their nannies or au pairs to be on duty on the party day. If the party is at a weekend, when she is not usually at work, make sure she knows about it well in advance, and that she hasn't got anything else planned. A lot of people think it is not fair to burden a hard-working nanny with this task outside her normal working hours; invite her to come by all means – your child will probably enjoy her presence and most nannies help once there – but don't be resentful if she declines. If you do ask her to be there in a working capacity, pay her extra for her time.

At least a week ahead, decide on the catering (see pp.28–37) and make a list of everything you need. Buy as much as possible as early as possible – you don't want to be flustered by a huge last-minute shop at the supermarket on the morning of the party. There may well still be things you forget which you can buy at the last minute, but these should be few. For your own sake, invest in disposable crockery, cutlery, tablecloths and napkins, especially for the younger age group: of course it works out more expensive, but think of that marvellous feeling of release as you tip the whole lot into a rubbish bag at the end of the party and chuck it in the bin! On the other hand, if you're having a sophisticated lunch party for your ten-year-old and a select few of his or her friends, let them use the best china and glasses and put flowers and candles on the table. They'll be so impressed that they'll be really careful.

Also a week ahead, decide on the games and prizes. Write out a list of possible games – it should have more ideas than you actually need – with alternatives for indoors if you're planning an outdoor party. Decide in advance which games are going to have prizes awarded and buy them, and then decide whether you're going to offer party bags or some other sort of going-home gift, and if so what it is going to consist of. This is why you must know exactly who is coming, because one of the thrills of party bags is to have the guest's own name on it.

Tail on the Donkey *is one of the many games for which advance preparation is essential.*

If you're going to have balloons and decorations you ought to decide what they are going to be in advance and allow enough time the evening before or on the morning to prepare and decorate the house. Decide where the main action is going to take place, and remove all breakables and unwanted furniture. You also need to have all the props ready for the different games in advance, and in a readily accessible place. It's no good saying to a group of excited six-year-olds 'Now we're going to play *Tail on the Donkey*,' and expect them to stand around quietly while you draw a donkey, find somewhere to pin it up and then make the tails. The descriptions of the games in this book tell you what you will need: look at them as you choose your games timetable and make sure you've got enough hats for *Musical Hats*, suitable music on cassette in a tape-player with a pause button for all musical games, at least two ready-wrapped parcels for *Pass the Parcel*, a thimble to hand for *Hunt the Thimble*, pencils and paper for *Heads, Bodies and Legs*, flags for *Flags in the Sand* and so on. And if you're going to be outside for part of the time, look carefully at the garden and site your race track away from your prize dahlias or whatever.

21

Suggested timetables

The timetables given here are only suggestions – ideas you can build on to fit your own circumstances and your child's preferences and age. But they will alert you to the sort of things you should be thinking about when planning ahead.

THREE-YEAR-OLD'S SUMMER BIRTHDAY TEA

This example assumes that you have (or have access to) a small garden.

One month before: Contact local gymtots group (these usually operate from your local leisure or sports centre) and arrange to hire suitable climbing equipment. Make sure you know whether they will deliver or if you are responsible for collecting, and if so when.

Two-three weeks before: Work out guest list and send out invitations.

One week before: Order the cake if you're not going to make it yourself. Buy all the party food except those things that need to be bought fresh on the day. If you can get ahead by making buns and freezing them etc., do so. (See pp.28–37 for ideas for food.)

Check the guest list to see who has definitely replied and ring round the others.

When you know more or less accurate numbers, buy party bags and little gifts and balloons, also disposable cups, plates and tablecloth.

Three days before: Make a list of party games and start searching the house for props so that you've got time to revise the list or go and borrow things from friends. As you are hiring climbing equipment, you will probably not need more than about half a dozen games but have a few more in reserve in case the weather turns bad.

Bake the cake.

The day before: Collect or take delivery of climbing equipment. Blow up balloons. Put party bags together. Make up parcels for *Pass the Parcel*. Collect together enough hats for *Musical Hats*. Draw a large tail-less donkey on a large piece of paper and cut out a good-sized tail for every guest, each with a name written on it. Find a suitable wall to stick up the picture at the right height for the children and put it in place.

Make sandwiches and cover with cling film, then keep in the fridge.

Defrost the buns; ice and decorate the cake; make individual jellies.

On the day: Decorate the house with balloons and streamers to taste. Set up the climbing equipment in the garden. Decide where you are going to have tea (indoors or out, depending on the weather) and check you've got enough chairs.

Cook the sausages; send your child out for a walk with a handy adult before lunch; have a light lunch and try to persuade your three-year-old to have a short rest, or at least a quiet time with a book. (Grandparents, if they are around, are often helpful with this important task.)

3.30 Guests begin to arrive. Supervise opening of presents and cards – it is almost impossible to stop a three-year-old from opening gifts immediately. Have someone on hand to retrieve them, they'll be discarded immediately in favour of the next parcel. Take the children out into the garden to chase bubbles while they wait for all the guests to arrive.

3.45 When almost all guests have arrived start playing games indoors; choose from:
  The Farmer's in the Den
  Ring-a-Roses
  Tail on the Donkey
  Pairs (pre-school version)
Play the games twice over if they seem popular.

4.15 Let the children go outside and play on the climbing equipment. Make tea for parents and other adults who have stayed for the party. While the children play, put out the party tea things.

Pass the Parcel is an absorbing but quiet game for youngsters to play after a filling birthday tea.

4.35ish Call the children to tea. Suggest a visit to the lavatory. Three-year-olds can be surprisingly good about eating birthday teas, especially if they have to sit at table, and this may well be quite a nice, quiet orderly moment.

4.50 Cake and 'Happy Birthday', plus blowing out the candles. Let the children get down from the table as soon as possible after this. Have a warm flannel ready for sticky faces and hands.

5.00 More games, outside so long as the weather is still fine:
  Pass the Parcel (to let their food go down!)
  Musical Hats
If *Musical Hats* gets out of hand (excited children do sometimes fight over this), switch to simple *Musical Bumps* instead.

5.15 Offer ice-creams in cones and let the children carry on playing on the climbing equipment until their parents come and fetch them or take them away at 5.30. Hand out party bags and balloons as the children leave.

SIX-YEAR-OLD'S CHRISTMAS PARTY

At least one month before (probably two or three): Book entertainer if required.

Three weeks before: Send out invitations (again the earlier the better – Christmas and New Year are popular times for parties and the children may have several to go to).

Persuade a suitable male friend to stand in for Santa Claus. Check size and book hire of costume from theatrical costumiers. (This may seem like a long time in advance, but Santa Claus costumes are very popular at this time of year!)

One week before: Prepare for the party as for three-year-old's above. Substitute little Christmas cake or a Yule Log for the birthday cake.

You'll need several games if you aren't going to have an entertainer.

The day before: Collect Santa costume with friend and arrange time of visit. Wrap small gifts and put in sack. (No party bags needed!)

On the day: You'll probably have decorated the house for Christmas anyway, but add balloons and have crackers round the tea table. Otherwise as for the three-year-old's party, only you don't have to take your six-year-old for a walk. Assign tasks to help – he or she will be only too pleased.

3.00 Guests arrive. Pin *Pairs* on backs as they come in. If the guests bring presents, put them under the Christmas tree – they are not to be opened until Christmas Day.

If you have hired an entertainer who needs time to set up, he or she will also probably arrive about this time.

3.15 Children find their partners. (A prize for the first pair to get together.)

24

3.20 Have a short *Wheelbarrow Race*, racing off two pairs at a time in heats.

3.30 *Musical Statues*. Give each child a particular character or animal perhaps to mime to the music to make it a bit more difficult, but make sure they keep moving about. Do this at least twice so that children who are slow to get going have a chance to join in fully.

3.45 Simple *Treasure Hunt*.

4.00 *Make Your Own Party Hat*.

4.15 Tea. End the meal with crackers and reading out the riddles.

4.40 Entertainer or a selection of games:
Grandmother's Footsteps
Heads, Bodies and Legs
Squeak, Piggy, Squeak
Oranges and Lemons (for ten or more)
Barmy Bowling
Sleeping Lions
The Hokey Cokey

5.20 Santa Claus comes to the door with his sack, and talks to the children, then gives out the small gifts from his sack. Follow with well-known carols round the Christmas tree until parents come to collect. It is nice to offer a glass of wine and a mince pie and suggest that parents join in the singing for a while, if they have time.

5.45ish The guests depart.

TEN-YEAR-OLD'S
MIDSUMMER GARDEN BARBECUE

Chin to Chin requires a surprising amount of skill, and played in boy-and-girl teams is a very good mixer.

In this example, the times for the actual party are approximate – play it by ear!

One month before: Decide on the date and time and, if appropriate, ring round mobile discos to find one suitable for your party. Discuss terms and suggest DJ comes to visit to decide on best position to set up.

Three weeks before: With your child, design and send out invitations. Decide on and stick to the guest list limit! (Fifteen to twenty is manageable in a reasonable-sized garden.)

One week before: Ring round to finalize actual numbers attending. Buy party food and freeze as much as possible. Think about house and garden decoration with your child and collect together appropriate decorative materials.

Buy a job lot of large white T-shirts or vests and a set of day-glo marker pens. Make sure you have plenty of old card.

Buy prizes for games if appropriate – consult with the DJ. You could order special badges or make rosettes to pin on lapels.

26

Two days before: Without your child around, work out clues for a *Treasure Hunt* and decide where they are going to be put.

The day before: Defrost burgers, buns, corn, sausages, and so on. Write out *Pairs* – do this with your child so that you get ones as relevant but as difficult as possible.

Before lunch: While your child decorates the house with help from other family members, pin up *Treasure Hunt* clues. Make sure you have pencils and paper for *What's on the Tray?*, put up poles in the garden for the *Wheelbarrow Slalom*, and find enough oranges for *Chin to Chin*.

3.30 - 4.00 Have the food, crockery, cutlery and glasses organized inside to avoid embarrassing delays later. Light barbecue. This may seem a little early, but it can take a long time to get the barbecue to the all-over even temperature that you need to cook the food, without charring it on the outside and leaving it raw in the middle – about two hours is safe. This means that the person doing the cooking can get on with it without hordes of starving ten-year-olds milling round and getting in the way. Also, since you will be cooking quite large quantities, and most domestic barbecues don't have very large capacities, the food itself will take a long time to cook, and you may need to keep some of it warm.

4.00 Guests start to arrive: give them a T-shirt and the day-glo markers and get them to design their own T-shirt and wear it for the party. When they've finished, pin half a *Pair* on their backs and give them another half to find.

4.30 When all children have paired off, run a *Wheelbarrow Slalom* race in heats of two or three pairs at a time, depending on how many poles you were able to put up. Have adults on hand to put up any poles that are knocked down.

4.50 *Chin to Chin*, in teams of four. Make the first and second pairs in the *Wheelbarrow Slalom* go first in each team – they probably won't be nearly so good at this game!

5.10 When the game's over, hand round drinks and snacks (crisps, peanuts, popcorn, and so on) and have everybody sit around while you have a *Twisters'* challenge – do this two at a time on the mat (see p.78) with the winner taking on the next challenger each time.

5.30 *Treasure Hunt* – this could take quite a lot longer than you think. Let the children work in pairs, chosen by writing down everyone's name and pairing off those with the most number of letters the same. As the children finish, get them to come in and play *What's on the Tray?*. This will require supervision to avoid cheating, if they're not doing it all at the same time. They must all have the same time limit to write down what they remember.

If it has not already done so, the mobile disco arrives and sets up. If it is set up, the DJ will probably arrive about now.

Depending on the maker's recommendations, start cooking the fries. Oven chips are easiest, since they can be cooked direct from the freezer and you don't need a deep-fryer, but this really is a matter of personal preference.

6.00 Start serving food. Remember that there will be a lot of milling about at this time, as the children collect their food and drinks.

6.15 Let the DJ take over and play music – he'll gradually draw the children in and dancing will begin. Save prize-giving for the games played earlier for the DJ to award, and get him to judge the best T-shirt design too.

7.30 - 8.00 DJ signs off and parents come to collect the guests. If the parents are a little early, offer them a drink too.

Planning the food

The centrepiece of a good children's party is always the food. It doesn't matter what time of the day or evening you are giving the party, always provide plenty to eat and drink. Children look forward to the party meal, and, unless you provide a buffet, it is the one time you can rely on them all being in the same place at the same time (useful if you feel the need to do a roll call!).

You can take the initiative in providing for young children's parties, but it is a good idea to involve older children in the preparation. What may surprise you is that they won't necessarily want junk food given the choice – a few tactful suggestions on your part will help to steer a middle way.

Tea parties for the under-eights

This is probably the easiest age group and type of party meal to cater for, and you can make it as simple or as elaborate as you like. The secret is variety, but not too much of anything at any one time. Young children do enjoy savoury snacks as well as sweet foods, but if you put them all down at the same time, they are inevitably going to choose the cakes and biscuits before the sausages and cheese pieces. The simplest and quickest way is to buy everything, so that food preparation is kept to the absolute minimum.

SAVOURY FIRST

Start by putting out small dishes of cocktail sausages or sausage rolls. Pre-cook both of these and let them cool down either to cold or lukewarm; it is not a good idea to serve them straight from the oven as children may burn their mouths (or their fingers) in the excitement. Do not use cocktail sticks for sausages as they too can cause nasty mouth injuries if children are rather excited and not thinking about what they are doing.

Pieces of Cheddar or Dutch cheese cut into cubes are often popular, although the practice of sticking them together with pieces of pineapple is a lot less popular with children of this age group than with adults. The advice about cocktail sticks applies here too. Potato crisps are always popular (try to find the low fat and lower salt types, and don't confuse matters by having flavoured crisps, stick to regular, ready-salted). Things like twiglets, small cocktail biscuits or cheese crackers, corn chips, hula-hoops (a huge favourite – expect several hands to be wearing ten rings at a time) also all go down well.

Some children like slices of cucumber or tomato, others enjoy slices of apple, orange or tangerine (they can usually peel their own), some even accept pieces of celery with cream or cottage cheese. If you know the group of children you are inviting well, you can ring round their parents to find out if there is anything they particularly like (or dislike). It is not advisable to offer peanuts to the under-threes, and some doctors would advise against them up to five years old. If a child chokes on a peanut, a substance in the nut reacts inside the child's immature lungs and can cause permanent lung damage.

SWEET SECONDS

Once the children have made reasonable inroads into the savoury selection, serve the plates of cakes and biscuits. Once again, don't provide too much of anything but have plenty of variety. If you offer chocolate biscuits (and why not?) have a warm flannel handy to wipe off the worst from faces and hands before it can be transferred to party clothes. If the children are very young, their parents will probably be there to see to this, but if you are giving a party for a group of six-year-olds, say, you will be doing their parents a favour if you send them home reasonably clean.

WHEN TO SERVE THE CAKE

If the party is for a birthday, Christmas, Easter or other religious festival you'll probably want to mark it by serving a special cake. When to present this is sometimes a bit of a problem, especially if you're also planning to serve jelly and ice-cream. It is probably best not to leave it right to the end of the tea party as the children may have started to become bored and certainly will have had too much to eat. Bring it in quite soon after you bring in the other cakes and biscuits, have the ceremonious blowing out of candles and cutting as appropriate and then serve *very small* pieces to everyone. Children love the idea of special cakes (see pp.35–7) but rarely eat them. Of course, there are the stalwarts who finish everything and want more – they are very rewarding to bake for – but most will be too full and too excited by this time to be bothered, so don't take it personally. Instead, arrange for a helper in the kitchen to cut up the cake and pack the pieces into foil or napkins to take home in the party bag.

JELLY ON A PLATE

If you still want to serve jelly or ice-cream, have it ready to serve immediately after the cake. Some children prefer it to cake anyway. A better solution is to save it till later. Clear away and then near the end of the party call the children back to the table for jelly and ice-cream or serve ice-cream in cones or wafers (especially for a summer party outside).

DOING IT YOURSELF

All the tea-party food mentioned can be bought at the supermarket (even the cake if you want) and as such will save you a lot of preparation time. You can also put out a little at a time and replenish the dishes that are most popular. (Expect to have several bags of crisps or whatever left over – there is always going to be one item which you over-supply, and one which runs out too quickly!) However, if you have the time and energy you can be a bit more adventurous.

Sandwiches need never be boring if the children cut them into fun shapes with pastry cutters.

Tea-time treats

SANDWICHES

Sandwiches were omitted from the list above deliberately, since they require preparation time. However, they do have a place on the tea-party table, so long as you don't make too many and don't expect all the children to eat them. Favourite fillings are egg mayonnaise, Marmite and peanut butter, with or without honey as well. Some children really enjoy fishy spreads like taramasalata (Greek smoked cod's roe spread) or canned tuna fish with mayonnaise. Ham is usually popular, but you could try salami or German sausage as well. Hard cheeses are best grated in sandwiches – small children sometimes find whole slices a bit challenging – alternatively, use cream cheese or cheese spread.

It is best to make the sandwiches small, and give your children a thrill by taking the crusts off! If you use soft, sliced bread you can cut the sandwiches into interesting shapes with pastry cutters – you'll be surprised how many more get eaten if they're shaped like hearts or flowers or teddy bears. It's fun to indicate the fillings with flags stuck into the top of the pile (use cocktail sticks for this but make sure you're the one to remove them when the time comes). If the children are too young to read, use a picture instead – although you might need some ingenuity to illustrate taramasalata!

An alternative to conventional sandwiches might be Scandinavian-style open sandwiches; with a little care you can make each one look like a face, and put a child's initial on it, using slices of cucumber, grated cheese, peas, even pieces of fruit.

PIES AND PASTRIES

Sausages and sausage rolls usually go down well and are a useful standby, but it is nice to provide something a little less predictable (you may in any case have vegetarian guests). Try individual quiches or little pasties. Children find these easy to hold, although be prepared for them to prefer the pastry to the filling!

SAVOURY QUICHES

For individual savoury quiches, make small fairly deep shortcrust cases, and bake them blind (as you would for a full-size quiche). Fill them with whatever you think your guests will accept – grilled bacon, grated cheese, tiny pieces of skinned tomato, slices of cooked courgette, sweetcorn, broccoli heads, flaked smoked fish, chopped ham, and so on.

Beat up two or three eggs with about three tablespoons of cream for every dozen quiches, then pour a little of this mixture over the filling, leaving at least 3mm (⅛in.) space at the top.

Bake in a medium hot oven (about 190°C/375°F/ Gas Mark 5) for 10–15 minutes until the egg is just firm and slightly browning on the top. Allow them to cool before serving.

SAVOURY PASTIES

Roll out shortcrust pastry and cut into rounds about 7–10cm (3–4 in.) in diameter. Again, fill them with whatever you think will go down well with your guests. You could try making traditional Cornish pasties with minced lamb, diced cooked potato and onion (although, like mushroom, this tends not to be very popular with under-sevens). More adventurous children may enjoy mildly spicy fillings like Jamaican patties. For these, add half a teaspoon of coriander, a sprinkling of turmeric for colour and half a teaspoon of garam masala (available from most supermarkets now) to a filling of potatoes, sweetcorn, peas and other acceptable vegetables.

Place a generous teaspoon of filling on one side (make the filling quite stiff so that it doesn't run out during the cooking), then fold the pastry over it, and pinch the sides together.

Place the pasties or patties on a greased baking sheet and bake at 180°C/350°F/Gas Mark 4 for 25–30 minutes, until the pastry is golden brown. Allow to cool slightly.

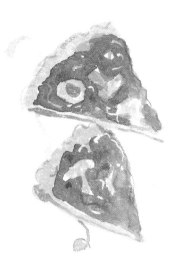

Some children enjoy small slices of thin crust pizza, but these aren't universally popular because so many are suspicious of olives, mushrooms and even onions if they are too visible. Your group of children may well be the exception, but avoid serving pizza without an alternative as well.

Another idea for the youngest age group is to provide each child with a lucky dip lunch box – a smallish box containing fun bits of food, like slices of raw carrot, pieces of cheese, raisins, small sweets, tiny novelty biscuits, cocktail sausages, slices of apple or peach or whatever fruit is in season, crisps, and so on. If you've got the patience, and there aren't too many guests, try wrapping some of the foods individually to make exciting little parcels to open. The food generally gets all muddled up on their plates when they help themselves – this way you make sure they all get a bit of everything!

Food for older children

Children of seven or eight and older usually have much more definite ideas about what they want to eat, so listen to them and make suggestions about what to provide. They will probably appreciate more adventurous ideas, like vegetable samosas, or Chinese spring rolls, or Turkish kebabs, or Greek pitta bread with fillings, or Malaysian pork satay (all of which can now be bought in the larger supermarkets and delis), rather than the more obvious hamburgers, hot dogs, chicken drumsticks or spare ribs. Don't reject these latter – at least you know they'll go down well – but you'll also be surprised by how receptive children still are to the conventional party tea. And at this age they can eat prodigious amounts so allow for this in the catering. Be a bit more adventurous with the sweet course too. Banana splits, ice-cream sundaes, strawberry shortcake and devil's food cake can all be handled with enthusiasm by older children. You can also provide interesting drinks, like a non-alcoholic fruit cup or cocktail, served up in cocktail glasses with stirrers and parasols for a good effect.

You can, of course, always take children of any age out to a fast food restaurant – most of the well-known chains welcome parties of children from two or three years upwards, so long as they are accompanied by adults. They will also often provide special hats and balloons and sometimes a clown or similar 'character' to sit with the children. You usually have to book ahead and give some idea of numbers and what you would like to order so that they can have enough ready over and above what they are serving all the time to their general customers.

The cake

If the meal is the centrepiece of most parties, the cake is the centrepiece of most meals. Even if it isn't a birthday celebration, children appreciate – indeed expect – some kind of special cake, which could be anything from a simple sponge to an ice-cream bombe. What you prepare depends on your own expertise and the amount of time at your disposal (you may prefer not to make your own cake at all). Many good bakers and confectioners make cakes to order, although the design of the icing may be limited. Many individuals also make cakes to order; these are often a much better bet as they are usually much more flexible in what they are prepared to do, and also very often cheaper. Ask around among your friends and neighbours to see if they know anyone who could do this – you never know, one of them may offer to do it themselves! Small-scale enterprises like these often advertise in the local press; alternatively look for notices in shop windows.

If you have never tried to make a novelty cake with a particular theme, the following simple ideas might help to start you off.

THE CAKE MIX

Although seasonal specialities have their place (such as rich fruit cake with marzipan and frosting for Christmas or spicy simnel cake for Easter), the average children's party cake is best made from a basic, simple sponge mix. One of the golden rules of children's parties is, they won't eat the cake! They'll think it's a wow, they'll want the first bit, or the slice with the Smartie, or the pink flower, or whatever, but only a small proportion of children actually eat a whole piece of party cake – they'll crumble it, lick the icing, pick off the chocolate buttons, but they are not actually eating it, just making a mess. And the younger the guests, the more likely this is. Most children are not that fond of fruit cake, and by the time the cake is served (see p.29) they won't really be hungry anyway.

PLAIN SPONGE MIX

255g (10oz) self-raising flour, and 2 tsp baking powder
255g (10oz) butter
255g (10oz) sugar
4 eggs

Put all these ingredients into a food processor or mixer and mix. The finished mixture should be firm but not too stiff (add a little milk if it is), smooth but not wet. Cook in a medium oven (180°C/350°F/Gas Mark 4) for about 45 minutes, or until the cake is lightly browned, springy to the touch and when a skewer inserted into the centre comes out clean.

The quantity given here is what you will need for most of these cake ideas, and as it is quite a substantial amount, it is worth using a food processor or mixer rather than spending a lot of precious time creaming the butter and the sugar, adding the eggs and then folding in the sifted flour. Borrow one if you haven't got your own.

You could add red food colouring to make a pink cake, or create a marbled effect by using a heaped teaspoonful of cocoa mixed with two teaspoonfuls of water dribbled into the mixture and then stirred in gently with a wooden spoon.

THE ICING

The ideas given here mostly use butter icing, which is good for building up shapes and cementing pieces of cake together, but glacé icing is also useful. About 450g (1lb) of made-up glacé icing is usually needed to coat most of these cakes, and about 675g (1½lb) of butter icing is needed to cover and decorate. It is probably sensible to make a little more than is necessary, and to buy an extra packet of icing sugar in case something goes wrong.

Most commercial food colouring is artificial, although you can obtain colourings based on natural products if you search for them. For a really technicolor cake, though, you are probably going to have to allow your child and his or her friends to indulge in some parentally introduced food additives – at least you can control the amount. If, however, you are unsure, check with your guests' parents particularly about yellow, which is usually made from tartrazine, which has been associated with hyperactivity. If in any doubt, leave it out.

GLACÉ ICING

450g (1lb) icing sugar
about 4 tbsp warm water
    and/or real lemon juice

Sieve the icing sugar into a bowl; this is really important as it makes it easier and quicker to work. Add the water a drop at a time, drawing the sugar in from the sides of the bowl with a fork, or use a food processor or mixer. The icing should coat the back of a spoon without dripping too quickly. Beat well. Add flavouring and colouring as required.

BUTTER ICING

450g (1lb) icing sugar
150–200g (6–8oz) softened
    unsalted butter
a little milk, if necessary

Beat the butter with a wooden spoon, then beat in the sieved icing sugar. This mixture will be very stiff, which is just right for building and modelling a cake, but if it is to spread over a cake, you might like to thin it down a little with about a tablespoonful of milk. Add flavouring and colouring as necessary. Remember that if you are adding, say, chocolate or coffee flavouring to make the icing brown, this will add fluid and therefore thin the mixture a little. You can always beat in a little more icing sugar to make it the desired consistency. Butter icing is very rich – if you are only adding tasteless food colouring, add a little real lemon juice as well to sharpen the taste slightly. Remember too that butter icing does not harden and will melt if it's allowed to get too warm!

EQUIPMENT

All these cakes are intended to sit on a large cake board – although a chopping board covered with aluminium foil does just as well and often gives you a bigger surface. You will either need a rectangular cake tin about 29cm × 22.5cm size (11½in. × 9in.), a round tin with a 22.5cm (9in.) diameter, a square tin 25cm × 25cm (10in. × 10in.) or a loaf tin 20cm × 12.5cm × 6cm (8in. × 5in. × 2in.). All tins take approximately 900g (2lb) of cake mixture, except the loaf tin, which takes about 675g (1½lb). You'll need a basic piping set too.

Cakes can be cut to any appropriate simple shape by tracing a picture on to greaseproof paper and then laying it over the cake. Make sure you cut with a sharp knife that will leave a clean edge. Save the pieces to build up extra features or details.

If you are already quite skilled at icing techniques you may well want to create the details of the different cake ideas with icing itself. For the less skilled or short of time (most of us), here is a list of useful accessories (most of them edible) to decorate your cake:

- Chocolate buttons for tiles, eyes, buttons etc
- Liquorice bootlaces for whiskers or tails
- Ice-cream wafers for windows, shutters or sails
- Smarties for decorative roof tiles, eyes, noses, flower centres, buttons etc (they are very versatile – but round jelly sweets are also a good alternative)
- Liquorice sweets (square or round) for windows, knobs, wheels
- Chocolate squares for windows or keys of a computer
- Coconut for grass
- Angelica for leaves
- Marzipan for making people, flowers, and so on.

FOOTBALL MATCH CAKE

Use a square or rectangular cake tin for this cake. Trim the cake, coat it with glacé icing and leave it to set overnight. This forms a good base for piping on to. When the icing is set, cover the cake with alternate stripes of light green and dark green butter icing to give the effect of a mowed pitch. Cover the sides with a thin layer of icing and then press halved chocolate finger biscuits along the sides as a fence. The line markings for the football pitch can then be beaded on using white glacé icing. Miniature footballers, goal posts, flags and so on, are available from novelty toy shops, model shops, or speciality cake and icing shops. Use a single Malteser for the ball.

COMPUTER OR TELEVISION CAKE

Use a square or rectangular cake tin, trim the cake and cut into two unequal pieces. The smaller piece is used for the computer keys. Scoop it out deep enough to place squares of chocolate in lines to represent the keys. Place both pieces of the cake in position on the cake board and cover the whole lot, including the gap in between, with glacé icing, then leave overnight to set. Pipe the screen of the computer in and put the chocolate squares in place. A good idea is to pipe the letters of the child's name on to the chocolate keys, and an appropriate greeting (Happy Birthday, Welcome Home, and so on) on the screen in computer lettering. If you want it to be a television set, you needn't cut the cake in two, but simply add chocolate squares or liquorice allsorts for control knobs or buttons either down the side of or underneath the screen area.

Designing and decorating the cake can be a joint effort for parents and older children.

ZOO OR JUNGLE CAKE

Again using a square cake, trim the edges and coat with glacé icing, then leave overnight to set. Scoop out an area of the cake almost to the bottom and place it on top to give the effect of stones or rocks. The scooped out area becomes a pond, so coat it with blue butter icing. The whole area above can be covered with green butter icing for the grass; colour shredded coconut green too to add texture. Cover the rocks or stones with brown or grey icing (use a little black food colouring). Cut chocolate finger biscuits in half and stand them all round to form a fence if it is to be a zoo. Trees can be made from pieces of green card cut to shape and slotted into the tops of chocolate fingers, or if you felt very resourceful you could perhaps make the leaves out of slices of angelica or the fresh leaves of herbs such as mint, lemon-scented verbena or geranium, or nasturtium. (Alternatively, use plastic model trees, obtainable from toy or model shops.) Chocolate buttons can be used for stepping stones across the pond and plastic zoo animals can be placed on the top among the trees or drinking from the pond.

LOG CABIN CAKE

This can be made in a loaf tin and a small square tin. If you want to make it Hansel and Gretel's gingerbread house, choose a ginger cake recipe, but don't use one that is going to be very moist – you could just add ginger flavouring to the basic sponge mix. Cut the square cake into two pieces and place these on the cake baked in the loaf tin to form the roof. Cover the cake with butter icing and the roof with chocolate flakes to represent logs. Use liquorice sweets and ice-cream wafers cut into shapes for windows and shutters and a piece of sponge for the chimney. Cover with butter icing and broken chocolate flakes pressed into place. If you feel confident, you might be able to make little Hansel and Gretel figures out of fondant or marzipan, or you could use models.

HOUSE CAKE

Use a square cake and cut it into the basic house shape. Cover the cake with glacé icing and leave to set overnight. The roof area can be covered with overlapping chocolate buttons or Smarties to look like tiles. Cover the walls of the house with butter icing (use cream, pale brown or pink colouring to make it look like a Suffolk cottage). Then either pipe in the windows using butter icing or use square liquorice sweets. Pipe in the door or use a sweet or a thin oblong of chocolate. You could also put flowers made from icing sugar around the edge and perhaps use lollipops for trees.

MOUSE CAKE

Make a basic sponge in a loaf tin, then cut out the basic shape of a mouse's body, as seen from above, using a sharp knife. Trim the cake into shape. Coat the cake with glacé icing and leave it to set overnight. Use butter icing for the actual mouse covering: pink is fun or you could make it white or even brown with white spots! Cover the mouse all over. For a pink or white mouse, use round pink liquorice allsorts for the eyes; other colours are probably best with black eyes. Use a blue or black liquorice sweet for the nose. Strips of liquorice can be used for the whiskers. Model the ears out of ready-made fondant or marzipan, or use marshmallows pushed into the cake. The mouse's tail too can be rolled out of fondant or marzipan coloured pink, or made from a liquorice bootlace.

This basic cake could be adapted for any simple animal shape – a cat, a tiger, even an elephant.

WINDMILL CAKE

Bake a rectangular cake and cut out the basic windmill shape without the sails. Save the cut-out pieces. Coat the basic cake with glacé icing and leave it to set overnight. Pipe the windmill with white butter icing. Make a door and windows out of remaining pieces of sponge and attach to the cake, then ice them appropriately. Make the sails from remaining pieces of cake as well, and pipe over with icing – you could stripe them with pale blue to give the effect of the sail boards.

Tips to make it go with a swing

Here are some basic organizational dos and
don'ts, and advice covering other aspects of
party-giving which perhaps in concentrating
on the occasion, the invitations, the food, and
the cake, you hadn't thought of but which can
hit you at just the wrong moment if
you aren't prepared.
There are lots of other tips to take
the wrinkles out of your preparation in all the
other sections of the book, and specifically
where relevant to the actual party games.

Practical hints

NUMBERS

Don't allow yourself or your child to get too carried
away with the number of children you invite.
Whatever your child would like, be realistic. The
younger the guests are, the fewer there should be
because too many children can be overwhelming
for all concerned and you will find more problems
of tears and tantrums before the end of the party.
For older children, it really does depend on your
own stamina and the amount of space and money
available. Many people find twelve to fifteen
children quite enough, and after the age of about
seven some people prefer to give up having
conventional parties at all, and arrange outings for
a few select friends (see pp.12–13).

DRAFTING IN HELP

Never embark on party-giving on your own, unless
it's for a group of under-twos who are all coming
accompanied by a responsible adult! A party is hard
work for a couple, let alone someone alone. You
can't concentrate on organizing and refereeing
games if you're worrying about setting the tea-
table, or having to dry someone's tears. You will
need at least one other person to help in the
kitchen, one person to organize the games and
another to be on hand to look after any shy or
difficult children, or cope with any unforeseen
problems. Don't be afraid to ask parents who are
staying at the party to help (they are usually glad
to have something definite to do).

AVOIDING SIBLING RIVALRY

If your child has older or younger brothers or sisters, it is important to consider their position in the party preparations. Older siblings can often dominate younger children's parties, and equally a younger child may not be able to keep up with older children's games and become frustrated and tearful, or simply get in the way. If the children are close in age, these problems probably won't arise, however, and if you're having some sort of general party, perhaps a Midsummer picnic or a Christmas party, you can usually mix the age groups quite successfully and divide the groups up for some games, if necessary.

For birthday parties, however, it really is a good idea to look at ways of making the party exclusive to the child whose birthday it is. If older children are at school, try giving a party at lunchtime for their pre-school sibling. Or arrange for the older child to go out with a particular friend on the understanding that when it comes to his or her turn, the younger child will be treated in a similar way. Another ruse is to let the older child or children invite one special friend each and then encourage them to help with preparations and organizing games rather than actually competing. This is guaranteed to make them feel important! Grandparents can be invaluable in entertaining a younger child – they could take him or her out at least for part of the time. The important thing is not to let the children feel they are being left out, but to stress that if they are patient, their turn will come all in good time.

TAKING CARE OF PETS

Pets often find large numbers of children frightening. Cats will usually make themselves scarce but if you live in a flat and your cat doesn't usually go out at all, shut your pet in one of the 'no go' rooms. Dogs can get rather over-excited so don't shut your dog in a room unless he's used to it. It's usually better to persuade a friend or neighbour to look after him for the duration of the party.

Caged pets like rabbits, hamsters or guinea pigs, can usually stay put, because they will just hide inside their hutches. Make sure, however, that younger children can't open the cage door easily. Caged birds should be placed out of reach, preferably in an unused room until after the party.

Children can be overwhelmed at first so provide a quiet place for shy guests.

SHY OR DIFFICULT CHILDREN

Among the younger age group there is often a child who is reluctant to join in because of shyness. Don't force him or her, but gently suggest the child joins in holding your hand. If this doesn't work just sit the child down quietly to watch, and keep drawing him or her into the games by including the child in any explanations. Perhaps the child might like to help by handing out prizes (this might make the games seem worth joining in) or help the person operating the cassette-player if you're having musical games. Have a quiet area with a few toys and books for children to 'sit out' in. Sometimes more than one child feels a bit overwhelmed at different times so this is always a useful resource — and it can come in

handy if any of the children are not happy about an entertainer or video you provide. Otherwise perfectly extrovert children can be shy if their parents stay at the party. In this case either leave the parents to sort it out, or if appropriate, find something practical for the parents to do which will take their attention away from their child, so that the child has the opportunity to focus more on what is happening at the party.

Aggressive or disruptive children are more problematic. You have to be quite firm right from the beginning and without losing your temper let it be known what is acceptable and what is not. If a child is spoiling the game for others by being pushy or cheating or just too boisterous, make the child sit it out, explaining in quite a friendly way that if he or she doesn't want to play it properly, then perhaps it would be better not to play at all. The problem may be just over-excitement during a very active game. If you think this is the case, cut the game short and play something quiet which requires concentration – *Sleeping Lions* (p.84) is a good one for almost all ages for this – and return to the active game later. Some disruptive children also respond to being given a responsible task, like helping with the cassette-player or using a stop watch or carrying things to the table for tea. Most wild behaviour is only the result of over-excitement and attention-seeking, so it's sometimes a good idea to single them out for special attention in this practical way.

PREPARING YOUR HOME OR GARDEN

If you are having the party in your own or someone else's home, there are practical considerations to take into account. Make sure 'no go' areas are clearly marked – if necessary lock doors to bedrooms, studies, workrooms, and garages (this is essential if they contain any dangerous equipment, and the same applies to the garden shed). Remove any valuable or breakable objects from the main areas where the party is to take place, and push back or remove unnecessary furniture. Take up rugs – they are bound to get rucked up and can be dangerous if covering polished floors. If you're worried about the dining-room carpet but you still want to have the meal in there, cover the floor with polythene sheeting or old dust sheets – none of your guests will mind!

In the garden, make sure garden pools are covered with mesh (this is a basic safety measure that everyone with small children should undertake, not just for a party), and if you have a swimming pool, even if it is to be used for part of the party, make sure it's not accessible the rest of the time. If you're worried about your prize chrysanthemums or the vegetable patch, rope areas off with tape, like workmen do when they're mending bits of the road. Bright day-glo tape will make it absolutely clear that you don't want anyone trampling about beyond its boundary.

41

About the games

GIVING PRIZES

Children under six can become very disheartened if they never win a prize at a party, and for this reason it is a practice to be avoided at this age: it undermines confidence and can make a child refuse to join in games because he or she never wins. Over the age of six children become increasingly competitive and prizes are appreciated. You can make them very small: buy a selection of novelties and wrap them individually and put them in a box. The winner then has to pick one out without knowing what it is. For sporty games and outdoor parties, make rosettes or badges to award the winners – that way you can give first, second and third as well. Another way to make sure everyone has a better chance of winning something is to award points for each game. For instance, if you are playing six games, you could award ten for each winner, eight for the second, five for the third and three for everyone else. Then add up all the points at the end and award prizes to everyone who scores over twenty points with a special prize for the highest three. You could also find unusual reasons for awarding prizes such as for being most helpful, or for being quietest at the party!

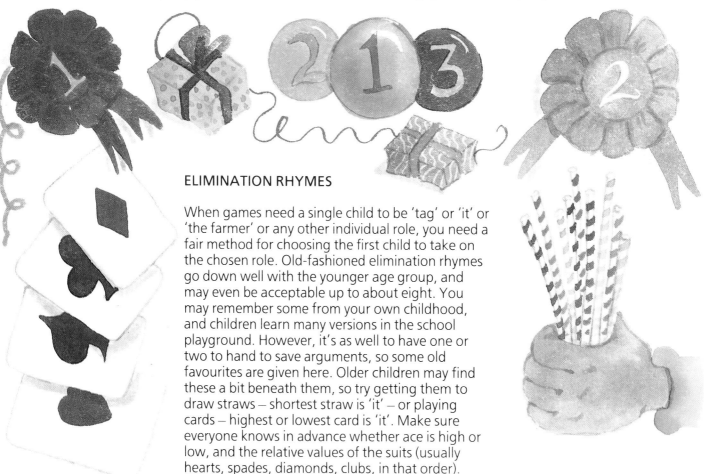

ELIMINATION RHYMES

When games need a single child to be 'tag' or 'it' or 'the farmer' or any other individual role, you need a fair method for choosing the first child to take on the chosen role. Old-fashioned elimination rhymes go down well with the younger age group, and may even be acceptable up to about eight. You may remember some from your own childhood, and children learn many versions in the school playground. However, it's as well to have one or two to hand to save arguments, so some old favourites are given here. Older children may find these a bit beneath them, so try getting them to draw straws – shortest straw is 'it' – or playing cards – highest or lowest card is 'it'. Make sure everyone knows in advance whether ace is high or low, and the relative values of the suits (usually hearts, spades, diamonds, clubs, in that order).

DIP, DIP, DIP

You point to each child in turn as you say each word, and the last child to be pointed at is the one chosen for the role.

*Dip, dip, dip,
My little ship,
Sailing on the water
Like a cup and saucer,
You are it.*

DIP, DIP

This works in the same way as Dip, Dip, Dip, *but it is short and to the point.*

*Dip, dip,
Sky blue
Who's it?
It's you.*

ONE POTATO, TWO POTATO

This takes longer than the other rhymes, but under-sevens enjoy it for its own sake. You need three or more children.

Everyone holds their hands out in front of them, fists clenched and thumbs upwards. These are the 'potatoes'. Make a fist yourself and as you say the rhyme, tap each fist in number order. When you get to the end of the verse ('more'), the child puts the hand you have just tapped behind his or her back. Repeat the rhyme and action until all the 'potatoes' except one have disappeared – the child with the last fist showing is chosen.

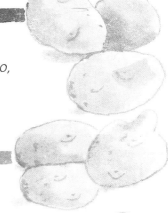

*One potato, two potato,
Three potato, four,
Five potato, six potato,
Seven potato, more.*

EENY MEENY

This is an up-to-date version of an old rhyme. Again, the last child to be pointed at is 'it'.

*Eeny meeny miney mo,
Catch a tiger by his toe,
If he hollers, let him go,
Eeny meeny miney mo.*

43

Music and movement games

Games involving music, singing, dancing and movement are popular with almost the whole age range, and are particularly useful for letting off steam at the beginning of a party. If there is a mixture of age groups, make sure there is plenty of room so that larger children don't knock over younger ones.

For games requiring music it is best to have taped cassettes or compact discs rather than records, which may get jogged. Also, most CD and cassette-players have a pause button. Choose continuous music that has a simple rhythm; the spaces between tracks can lead to misunderstandings. These games need two helpers – one to play the music, one to referee.

Games with music

MUSICAL BUMPS

Age 2 – 6

Although this simple game is ideal for children from as young as two up to six years old, they get very good at it by about five and you may have to introduce forfeits to sort out dead heats. It is suitable for indoors or out though you need to use a fairly large room cleared of furniture and floor rugs, and if you're playing outdoors you may need to play music loud, so warn the neighbours first!

Play a suitable musical tape while all the children run, dance or jump about. (Younger children always seem to jump on one spot.) The person operating the tape-player stops the music suddenly using the pause button; the children should sit or bump down on to the floor immediately. The last child to sit down is out; he or she should sit out and help you decide who was the last in the next round. The last child left in after all the others have been eliminated wins.

MUSICAL STATUES
Age 4-6

This is more difficult for the very youngest children, so it is probably best kept for the over-fours.

Play taped music as for *Musical Bumps* while the children run or dance about. When the music stops, the children should freeze like statues in the exact position they were in when the music stopped. Any child who moves or wobbles is out. Keep playing until all the children but one have been eliminated. For this game, make sure the children do keep running or dancing – jumping up and down makes 'freezing' too easy.

MUSICAL CHAIRS
Age 3-7

Make sure you choose chairs that are a suitable height for the average size of the guests.

Set out a line of chairs, one less than the number of children playing, facing alternate ways. While the music plays, the children run or dance round the line of chairs without touching them. When the music stops they must sit down quickly on a chair – the child left without a chair is out. Remove one chair, and continue to play rounds until only one chair and two children are left. The one who sits on it when the music stops for the last time wins.

ANIMAL STATUES

This is a variation of *Musical Statues* for six- and seven-year-olds. Start to play in the usual way, but when the music stops, the children have to 'freeze' into the shape of different animals – either give them individual ones before the game starts, or choose an animal for all of them for each round.

MUSICAL HATS

Musical Hats is like *Musical Chairs*, except that the children dance around a pile of hats in the middle. When the music stops, each child has to put on a hat from the pile. At the end of each round put one less hat back into the pile. Make sure you use old hats as this game can lead to some quite hard tugging!

HAT PARADE
Age 5+

This is a combination of Musical Hats *and* Musical Chairs *which avoids the usual scramble that ensues when the music stops in both of these more traditional games; it is none the less fun.*

Place enough chairs in a circle, all facing the same way, so that every child taking part has a chair to sit on. Give all the children except two some sort of hat to wear, anything will do so long as it is a proper piece of headgear. The two children without hats should be sitting at opposite sides of the circle of chairs. When the music starts each child takes off his or her hat and passes it on to the person in front, and in turn takes the hat from behind. The children must put the hats on their heads properly before passing them on to the next child. (The hats in fact go round and round the circle, rather than the children going round and round the hats!) When the music stops the two children left without hats are out. Remove their chairs, close up the circle a bit, and remove two more hats. At the end of the game there will be two children left with hats – either make them joint winners or allow a 'sudden death' play-off with one hat between the two, with the children sitting on chairs one behind the other.

UNDERNEATH THE ARCHES
Age 5-8

This is a rewarding game for most children because even when someone is 'out', he or she doesn't have to sit around doing nothing while the rest of the players finish the game. For obvious reasons, it's no good for small parties.

Divide the children into pairs (use one of the pairing games given on p.115 if you like). Choose two pairs to form arches with their hands raised (as for *Oranges and Lemons,* see p.49), and get them to stand at either end of the room. When the music plays, the pairs hold hands and dance one after the other round the room and under the arches (they must do this or they will spoil the game). When the music stops the children forming the arches have to capture any pairs (or part of a pair) that is passing under the arch at that moment. The captured pairs form another arch which the remaining children have to pass through as well in the next round. Continue the game until all the pairs have formed arches. (You may well find there are no clear winners in this game; when, say, only two couples are left dancing round and everyone else has formed arches it is very difficult for the dancing couples to escape.)

ARM IN ARM
Age 6-10

Any group of children can play this game, but it is a particularly good one for breaking the ice between boys and girls at a mixed party in the older age group, and is even suitable for the over-tens.

Divide the children into two groups, with one group having one more person than the other. (If you've got an even number, then an adult will have to stand in for a while.) Line up the slightly smaller group down the centre of the room, one in front of the other, each with a hand on his or her hip and the elbow crooked out. Alternate between right and left arms down the line. When the music starts, the other group dance or run round the line until the music stops, at which point they all try to link arms with the child nearest to them. The person left without an arm to link up to is out. Remove a child from the centre line too (the one at the front or the back, or whatever – alternatively let the 'out' child choose another to be out with him or her). Carry on until two children are contesting for only one.

FOR OLDER CHILDREN

If you want to use *Arm in Arm* as a good way to get boys and girls to mix at a pre-teen party, make each team consist of all girls and all boys. Alternate which sex stands with arms on hips, and which run round and try to link up.

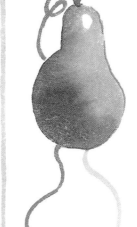

Singing games

RING-A-ROSES
Age up to 5

This game can be played indoors or out.

The children should stand in a circle holding hands (include one or two adults if toddlers are taking part). Skip round singing the song and when you sing 'Down!', everyone sits or lies down. Crouch down to sing the second verse, and when you sing 'Up!' everyone jumps up as high as they can.

*Ring-a-ring o' roses
A pocket full of posies
Atishoo! Atishoo!
We all fall down.*

*Picking up the daisies,
Picking up the daisies,
Atishoo! Atishoo!
We all jump up!*

THE TRAIN IS A-COMIN'
Age up to 5

For this game, you can sing the words of any train song that has a good railway rhythm such as 'The Train Is a-Comin'' or 'The Runaway Train'.

Line up all the children one behind the other, and get them to hold on to each other at the waist or at the shoulders (not both!). They are the coaches. Choose an adult (or an older child) to be the engine and train driver in one. Back the engine up to the first 'coach' and couple on, then begin to draw out of the station slowly in time to the music, either sung or chanted. The idea is to snake round, moving fast then slowly without the train breaking up behind the engine. The adult has to remember to take small steps as the children's legs are much shorter, and don't forget the train whistle or hoot!

THE STEAM TRAIN

An alternative to singing *'The Train Is a-Comin''* or another train song, is to chant like a steam train chuffing out of a station, slowly at first, then gathering speed:
*Coff-ee Coff-ee
Tea and biscuits
Tea and biscuits
Fish and chips
Fish and chips
Sou-oup! Sou-oup!*

ORANGES AND LEMONS
Age 5-7

This traditional rhyming game is best played with quite a large group, with two of the tallest children forming the 'bridge'. Keep an eye on the length of the two teams so that the tug of war at the end isn't too one-sided.

Choose one child to be oranges and another lemons (but keep this a secret so that the other children don't know which is which). The two children hold both hands in a high bridge which the other children run round and under while singing the main part of the song. When they get to the chanted chorus — 'Here comes a candle to light you to bed, and here comes a chopper to chop off your head!' — the children dash through quickly. On the last 'chop' the two children bring their arms down quickly to capture the child going through, then ask the child whether he or she wants to be oranges or lemons. The child whispers the answer so that the other children still can't discover which is which and then goes and stands behind the chosen child. When all the children have been captured and there are (hopefully) more or less the same number on each side, everyone holds on round the waist of the child in front. When you say 'Go', the two groups have a tug of war to see whether oranges or lemons are stronger. Since everyone usually tumbles to the floor no matter what, the game ends in hilarious confusion.

(Sung:)
Oranges and lemons
Say the bells of St Clements
I owe you five farthings
Say the bells of St Martin's
When will you pay me
Say the bells of Old Bailey
When I grow rich
Say the bells of Shoreditch
When will that be
Say the bells of Stepney
I do not know
Says the great bell of Bow.

(Chanted:)
Here comes a candle to light you to bed,
And here comes a chopper to chop off your head!
Chop . . . chop . . . chop . . . CHOP!

IN AND OUT THE DUSTY BLUEBELLS
Age up to 8

This is a very good singing game for a mixed group of children up to about eight years old, although probably a group of seven- or eight-year-olds on their own might feel it's a bit juvenile. It's a good idea to have two or three adults involved as well, as the children enjoy watching them having to bend down, and the end of the game (when there are only two people left) is more interesting if two adults can form an arch.

The children (and adults, if appropriate) form a large circle and hold hands, lifting them up high to form arches. Choose one child to start going 'in and out the dusty bluebells'. As everyone sings the first verse of the song, he or she weaves in and out of the circle ducking under the arched hands. At the end of the chorus, the child chooses one of the circle to join him or her, tapping the child's shoulder while everyone sings the second verse. As everyone starts to sing the first verse again, the second child holds on round the first child's waist and they both weave in and out. When they get to the second verse again, the second child chooses a third to join the 'snake', and so on until all but two of the circle have been chosen. The two last people form the arch, then everyone sings the first verse one last time as they form a snake weaving a figure of eight under and round the arch.

(Sung to the tune of 'Bobby Shafto'):
In and out the dusty bluebells,
In and out the dusty bluebells,
In and out the dusty bluebells,
Who will be my partner?

Tippy, tippy, tap tap on your shoulder,
Tippy, tippy, tap tap on your shoulder,
Tippy, tippy, tap tap on your shoulder,
You will be my partner.

50

THE FARMER'S IN THE DEN

Age up to 5

A good game to start a party with, this traditional singing game is a great standby for the under-fives who will play it happily several times over without getting bored. Five- to seven-year-olds find it reassuringly familiar too, making it ideal for mixed-age-group parties.

Choose a child to be the farmer. All the other children join hands, with the farmer in the middle. They circle round the farmer for the first verse, after which he chooses another child to be the wife. All the children circle round the pair for another verse, then the wife chooses a child, and so on. Some versions of the game suggest that at the end everyone pats the dog (gently) on the head, others that everyone pats the bone, others still that everyone pats the whole family!

The farmer's in the den,
The farmer's in the den,
Ee-I-addio
The farmer's in the den.

The farmer wants a wife,
The farmer wants a wife,
Ee-I-addio
The farmer wants a wife.
(Choose a wife)

The wife wants a child,
The wife wants a child,
Ee-I-addio
The wife wants a child.
(Choose a child)

The child wants a nurse,
The child wants a nurse,
Ee-I-addio
The child wants a nurse.
(Choose a nurse)

The nurse wants a dog, etc
(Choose a dog)

The dog wants a bone, etc
(Choose a bone)

We all pat the dog/bone, etc

LOST LETTERS

Age 5-7

This is a good game for a group of children to play indoors as it allows them to run about, but only two at a time. You probably need at least ten children so that you get a decent-sized circle for them to race round.

All the children but one sit in a circle facing inwards. Give the child outside a letter – it could be a real envelope or a handkerchief or scarf. He or she walks or dances round the outside of the circle while singing the song, to the tune of 'Simple Simon'. If the child doesn't want to sing, he or she can simply say the words; alternatively, get all the children to sing.

I sent a letter to my love,
And on the way I dropped it,
One of you has picked it up,
And put it in your pocket.

The child then walks quickly or skips round the circle pointing to each child while chanting, 'It isn't you, it isn't you, it isn't you, it isn't you . . .' until he or she decides to drop the 'letter' in the lap of the chosen victim and says 'It's you!'. The chosen child jumps up and both children race round the outside of the circle in opposite directions to see who can get back to the empty space first. The child who is left standing has the next turn at taking the letter round the circle.

FOR MIXED AGE GROUPS

If you want to play *Lost Letters* with a group of children of different ages, and think that the smallest ones will lose out too often if they have to run, suggest different ways of racing round such as crawling or bunny-hopping.

This can also be a useful alternative if you think that you don't really have enough space for two children to run around the outside of a large group.

52

THERE'S A PIGEON IN MY POCKET

Age up to 9

This is a variation of Lost Letters. *As it involves tagging as well as racing back to the vacant place, you need lots of room to play. It isn't a good game to play with a group of mixed ages as the smaller ones may lose out too often and become upset.*

Everyone sits in a circle well spread out. Choose a child to be the first person to sing the song. Holding a small object such as a pen or comb, he or she runs or skips round the outside of the group singing or chanting the rhyme.

*There's a pigeon in my pocket,
But it won't bite you,
Won't bite you,
Won't bite you,
There's a pigeon in my pocket,
But it won't bite you,
But it will bite you!*

As the child runs round, he or she pretends to drop the object behind each child until the last line of the rhyme when he or she does actually drop it behind one of the seated children and then dashes on round the circle to try and get back to the vacant place. The 'bitten' child jumps up at the same time, grabs the object and tries to catch the first child before he or she can run round and sit in the space left by the child who was 'bitten'. Unlike *Lost Letters,* the children run round the circle in the same direction. If the child with the 'pigeon' sits down in the vacant space first, then the 'bitten' child has the next turn as pigeon. If not, the same child takes a turn as pigeon again.

IF YOU'RE HAPPY AND YOU KNOW IT

All ages

Everyone can play this singing and action game, because you can suit the difficulty of the actions to the age of the children. This is a good game to finish off with, either just before tea or before going home.

All the children stand in a circle and follow either the actions suggested by the adult leader, or take it in turns to suggest actions themselves.

*If you're happy and you know it
Clap your hands!
If you're happy and you know it
Clap your hands!
If you're happy and you know it,
Then surely you should show it,
If you're happy and you know it,
Clap your hands!*

Actions for younger children could include 'Stamp your feet'; 'Nod your head'; 'Turn around' and 'Swing your arms/legs'.

Actions for older children could include 'Wink an eye'; 'Stand on one leg'; 'Stand up, sit down'; 'Go to sleep'; 'Jump up high'; 'Crouch down low'; 'Stand on your hands' and 'Forward roll'.

HERE WE GO ROUND THE MULBERRY BUSH

Age up to 5

Another favourite! Ask older children to suggest actions when you run out of ideas yourself.

The children hold hands and dance round in a circle for the chorus. The leader (either an adult or a child who knows the game well) then sings the verse, including an action which all the children copy. Everyone dances and sings the chorus again, before going on to the next action verse. This game can continue for as long as the children are interested, but four verses are probably enough for the very youngest children.

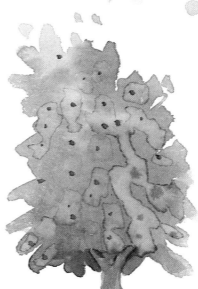

Here we go round the mulberrry bush,
The mulberry bush, the mulberry bush,
Here we go round the mulberry bush
On a cold and frosty morning.

This is the way we wash our hands,
Wash our hands, wash our hands,
This is the way we wash our hands
On a cold and frosty morning.

Here we go round the mulberry bush, etc

This is the way we wash our face,
Wash our face, wash our face,
This is the way we wash our face
On a cold and frosty morning.

Here we go round the mulberry bush, etc

This is the way we brush our teeth,
Brush our teeth, brush our teeth,
This is the way we brush our teeth
On a cold and frosty morning.

Here we go round the mulberry bush, etc

This is the way we fall on the floor,
Fall on the floor, fall on the floor,
This is the way we fall on the floor
On a cold and frosty morning.

(This is a very good way to end the game when ideas are running out!)

WHO WILL COME IN?

Age up to 5

Who Will Come In? *is sung to the same tune as* Here We Go Round the Mulberry Bush, *but is just a simple dancing game without any other actions. At the end, when all the children have been chosen, they form one large ring, holding hands.*

The children stand in a circle round one child while singing the first verse of the song, 'Who will come in to my small ring?'. At the end of the verse the child in the centre points to one of the children round him or her. This child answers 'Me, me', then joins hands with the child in the middle and they both dance round while all children sing the next verse. Continue the game until all children have been chosen.

Who will come in to my small ring,
My small ring, my small ring?
Who will come in to my small ring
And make it a little bit bigger?

Chosen child: *Me! Me!*

Who will come in to my small ring,
My small ring, my small ring?
Who will come in to my small ring
And make it a little bit bigger?

HEADS, SHOULDERS, KNEES AND TOES

All ages

This well-known action song can be adapted for different age groups. Older children particularly usually enjoy the suppressed excitement of the 'dumb' version!

If you are playing with under-fives, simply get them to touch the parts of the body with both hands as they sing or say the words. Start slowly and gradually speed up until everyone is thoroughly muddled.

*Heads, shoulders, knees and toes,
Knees and toes,
Heads, shoulders, knees and toes,
Knees and toes,
And eyes, and ears, and mouth, and nose,
Heads, shoulders, knees and toes!*

For older children, start off singing all the words and touching the parts of the body to get into the song. Then, gradually leave out each part, continuing to think it and touch the part of the body, *and* keep the rhythm of the tune.

****** shoulders, knees and toes,
Knees and toes,
***** shoulders, knees and toes,
Knees and toes,
And eyes, and ears and mouth and nose,
***** shoulders, knees and toes!*

Gradually speed up, leaving out each part of the body in turn. In the last round you should be thinking and miming the whole song in silence. You can end up with a really fast loudly sung complete verse again so that everyone can let off steam after keeping quiet and having to concentrate for such a long time.

Dancing games

THE CONGA
Age 6+

Traditionally, this is used to end a party or dance, and as such it's a good way of occupying young people while they wait for parents to come and fetch them. Children younger than about six might need help from adults to avoid being left behind. It is best for the older age group so long as the leader knows his or her way around, and where not to go!

All you need is music with a Latin rhythm. Everyone forms a long snake one in front of the other, holding on to the child in front round the waist or on the shoulders. In time to the music, the leader sets off with three steps then a kick, then three more steps and a kick with the other leg. The Conga line should all step and kick in formation, though in practice they often get out of synch, leading to much hilarity. The leader snakes the Conga through the whole party area (preferably house and garden — and even into the street with supervision), weaving in and out of doors and furniture as slinkily as possible.

THE PAUL JONES
Age 10+

If you are giving a pre-teens' disco or barn dance, the disc-jockey or caller will probably find ways of getting the children to mix. It is sometimes difficult for parents organizing their own events for the older age group to achieve this without some (fairly) subtle strategies – ten- and eleven-year-olds nowadays may consider themselves far too sophisticated to be manipulated into mixing, especially boys with girls. Try this if you think the division of the sexes is getting too entrenched. It can be danced equally well to country dance music or pop music.

Get the children to form two large circles one inside the other, facing each other, and holding hands. (You need an even number of children in each ring – preferably all boys on the outer ring and all girls on the inner. If you have an odd number, get an adult to join in, too.) While the music plays the two circles of children dance round in opposite directions. Stop the music at random, as for *Musical Bumps* or *Statues*. The boy and girl facing each other when the music stops then dance the next dance together, if appropriate. (You could equally well use the Paul Jones as a good way for older children to form pairs for other games, such as a three-legged race.) Then resume the Paul Jones formation to create new partners for the next dance or game.

THE HOKEY COKEY
All ages

Even the most sophisticated ten-year-old will enjoy this cockney favourite. It is particularly good for a mixed-age-group party, especially if there are several adults present, and children from three upwards can join in for a good knees-up!

Everyone joins hands in a big circle (if there isn't room, form two lines facing each other, each line holding hands). During the chorus everyone swings their arms up and into the middle (or the lines come towards one another), and then swings back; otherwise, follow the movements of the verses.

*You put your left leg in
You put your left leg out
In, out, in, out, shake it all about.
You do the hokey cokey and you turn around,
That's what it's all about!*

*Oh–oh, the hokey cokey!
Oh–oh, the hokey cokey!
Oh–oh, the hokey cokey,
Knees bend, arms stretch, ra! ra! ra!*

*You put your right leg in
You put your right leg out
In, out, in, out, shake it all about.
You do the hokey cokey and you turn around
That's what it's all about!*

Chorus

*You put your left arm in
You put your left arm out
In, out, in, out, shake it all about.
You do the hokey cokey and you turn around
That's what it's all about!*

Chorus

*You put your right arm in
You put your right arm out
In, out, in, out, shake it all about.
You do the hokey cokey and you turn around
That's what it's all about!*

Chorus

*You put your whole self in
You put your whole self out
In, out, in, out, shake it all about.
You do the hokey cokey and you turn around
That's what it's all about!*

Chorus

Drawing and collage games

Children of any age can enjoy any of these activities if you scale them to the right level of ability. Under-sixes will need quite a lot of adult assistance with most of them, but it's rewarding to see how much pleasure they get from games that involve making something for themselves.

Colourful accessories

MAKE YOUR OWN PARTY HAT

Age 3 – 8

Not so much a game as an activity, this is very popular with children of most ages, so long as there is plenty of help (in particular, to use the scissors and lend a hand with the glue) for the younger age group and plenty of materials available for all – you can't over-estimate how much they'll use! It is a good idea to arrange to do this just before you intend to have the party meal so that everyone can wear their hat during it. Older children could have a hat parade and you could award little prizes for the silliest, brightest, tallest, and so on. Don't let them know beforehand what your categories are or you'll have everyone competing for the easiest to comply with. You can also improvise on the categories according to what you are presented with so that in fact everyone gets a prize of some sort.

You'll need to provide a wide variety of coloured paper, card, stickers, scissors, glue, sticky tape, tissue paper, maybe some pieces of fabric, bottle tops or aluminium foil, straw, wool – anything that can be stuck on to the basic card shape to decorate a hat. For the smallest age group cut out bands – either straight or with points like crowns – and provide felt-tip pens and coloured paper shapes. Older children will probably want to cut out their own card shapes. Sticky tape is best for fixing the card to the correct head size, alternatively an adult could staple the ends together.

DESIGN YOUR OWN T-SHIRT
Age 7-10

Again, more of an activity than a game, this is good for a group of older children, and gives them something interesting and creative to take home as a keepsake.

Provide each child with a white T-shirt. You might be able to buy these cheaply in a market, or perhaps obtain some secondhand (give them a wash and bleach first). It doesn't matter if they are too big – if they are, the children will have more space to be creative. Provide a selection of felt-tip markers with indelible ink. (These can be obtained from art and design suppliers.) Bright primary colours and black are best, and some day-glo or hi-liter ones also add to the fun.

Make sure too that each child has a large piece of card to put inside the T-shirt so that the design does not go through to the other side, then let your artists' imaginations run riot over the front and back. Everyone can then wear their T-shirt for the rest of the party.

NEWSPAPER DRESSING UP
Age 7-10

This is an ingenious race for creative children. Because it requires the use of staplers and scissors, it has to be confined to the older age group. The game has to be played in pairs or teams because the garments can only successfully be created on the body of one of the children.

Divide the children into pairs, or introduce this game after the children have been paired off in one of the ways described on p.115. Supply each pair with a pile of old newspapers (broadsheet is more versatile than tabloid size), a roll of sticky tape, a stapler and a pair of scissors. When you say 'Go', or blow a whistle, the children have to create a suit for one of the pair – jacket and trousers or a skirt – out of newspaper held together with staples and sticky tape. The first pair to be ready wins.

If you have quite a number of children and don't have enough equipment to supply all the pairs, divide the children into teams and get them to 'dress' an adult, one per team.

Drawing games

TRACE THE SHAPE

All ages

This is a simple race which can be adapted to different age groups, by choosing simple or complicated shapes.

Provide everyone with tracing paper, a soft pencil or crayon (depending on age), and pictures to trace from. Very simple outline shapes are suitable for the three-to-fives, but older children can have quite complicated pictures from magazines to trace (make it more difficult by telling them only to trace certain objects in each picture). Then simply start the race in the usual way: no pencils on the paper until you say 'Go', or blow a whistle, and then give them two minutes to do as much as they can, blowing the whistle or shouting 'Stop' when time is up. Ability is often wildly varied at this so it might be better not to give prizes – although you could perhaps offer a prize for the neatest trace as well as to the child who has done most.

Older children could be given a space on a wall to tape up their efforts once done, to be included in the race time (allow a bit more)!

FACE PAINTS

Although not strictly a game, face paints are always popular. Painting the children's faces as they arrive is a good way of starting things off, but put a towel round them while you're doing it to avoid getting any paint on party clothes. Although most manufacturers claim that face paints are washable, in practice some of the stronger colours can be difficult to wash out of clothes. You could give older children a set of face paints and a mirror so that they can do it themselves.

NAMING THE DRAWING

For an older age group playing *Heads, Bodies and Legs*, it can be funnier still if, after finishing the drawing and passing it on, the children leave enough room at the bottom to write the name of the person they think the drawing represents (for example, Mum, Superman, my teacher, Skeleton, Grandad, Michael Jackson). They then fold over the paper again and pass the drawings on for opening – everyone reads out the name of the portrait they are holding before showing it off.

HEADS, BODIES AND LEGS

Age 5+

This is a good quiet game for a mixed age group of children over five, which is the age when almost all children can feel confident about differentiating the parts of the body in the required way.

Give everyone a piece of paper and a pencil. First of all, everyone draws a head and neck, making it as silly or funny as they want. (It is important that they don't let anyone else see what they are doing.) Then they fold the paper over so that only the end of the neck shows through, and pass their paper on to the next person (establish which way round you're going first). The next child draws the body down from the neck to the top of the thighs, joining it on to the neck showing below the fold. Once again everyone folds his or her paper to hide the body, leaving only the tops of the thighs showing, and passes the paper round again. The next child draws the legs, knees and feet. Then everyone folds down the whole drawing and passes the papers on once more, before everyone opens the drawing they are holding, producing a hilarious portrait gallery of very silly people.

Word games

Word games have the advantage of being absorbing and (mostly) quiet – they provide an opportunity for a break between very active games, or perhaps just before serving a meal. There are games to suit all age groups, they don't all require reading and writing skills. For those that do need pencil and paper, make sure you have enough paper and pens or pencils ready – children at parties don't have the patience to sit quietly while you scrabble in the back of a drawer, only to find two more worn-out felt-tips.

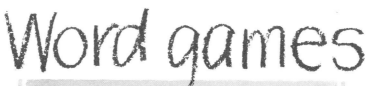

Spoken word games

MY GRANDMOTHER WENT TO MARKET
Age 5 –10

There are several variations of this basic and fairly simple memory game. The older the children are, the better their memories will be, and the longer the game will last.

Get the children to sit in a circle or group. The first child says something that grandmother may have bought, for instance, 'My grandmother went to market and bought some fish.' The next child says, 'My grandmother went to market and bought some fish and some potatoes.' The next child says,

'My grandmother went to market and bought some fish, some potatoes and a pair of tights.' The fourth child says, 'My grandmother went to market and bought some fish, some potatoes, a pair of tights and a bicycle repair kit', and so on round the group. Each person has to list everything that has gone before, as well as adding their own item of shopping to grandmother's basket.

Anyone who misses something out or gets any of the items listed in the wrong order is out; the person who remembers everything in the right order for longest wins. Of course, the quotes here are only examples – the children can make their grandmother buy anything they choose so long as it is a real, and not made up, item.

ALPHABETICAL VERSIONS

These variations on *My Grandmother* make it even more difficult!

In the first, the items bought must be listed in alphabetical order, for example, 'My grandmother went to market and bought some apples'; 'My grandmother went to market and bought some apples and a bicycle'; 'My grandmother went to market and bought some apples, a bicycle and a carpet', and so on. It gets tricky around x, y and z!

In the second, the items bought must all begin with the same letter, changing letters after each child has had a turn. In the first round, it might be 'My grandmother went to market and bought some apples'; 'My grandmother went to market and bought some apples and an amplifier'; 'My grandmother went to market and bought some apples, an amplifier and an anteater' and so on once round all the children. When you get back to the first child, they have to list all the things beginning with 'a', then start with things beginning with 'b'.

I FLEW TO TIMBUKTU
Age 6 - 10

This is really the same game as My Grandmother Went to Market *in a different context – but it can allow older children to indulge in extraordinary flights of fancy.*

The children sit in a circle again as for *My Grandmother Went to Market*. This time the preamble is 'I flew to Timbuktu and in my suitcase I packed a . . .' and the first child has to say something beginning with 'a'. The next child has to say something beginning with 'b' and so on round the group. Once again, it requires a lot of ingenuity towards the end of the alphabet as the children have to remember everything that has gone before, and think of something beginning with 'x' or 'z'.

DEFINITIONS

Age 8 - 10

This traditional word game is another which has been turned into an upmarket TV quiz game for adults, but children still enjoy it, and it's a very good game for a mixed party of children and adults, such as at Christmas. It is best played by a smallish group, so that there are perhaps four in each team.

Divide the children into two teams. One team goes out of the room with the biggest dictionary you can find and looks up a very peculiar word. The children write down the correct definition and make up other definitions, one for each child, as well. (If the children are playing on their own, they may need a few suggestions from an adult.) The team then goes back into the room and reads the definitions out to the other team, which has to guess which is the right one. If the opposing team guesses right they score a point, if they get it wrong the defining team wins a point. Then the teams change sides, with the second team going out of the room to choose a word and making up other definitions in turn. Have three or four rounds, or as many as the children can manage without losing concentration; the team with most points at the end wins.

TELEGRAMS
Age 7–10

This traditional word game can be played either verbally – if the words are not too long – or using pencil and paper.

Think of a word of between six and twelve letters (anything longer than six really needs to be written down). In turn, the children then have to make up telegram messages using words beginning with the letters of the chosen word in the right order. As telegrams aren't used much any more, you may have to explain that they can use 'telegrapheze', shortening the sentences to leave out words like 'a', 'the', 'I', 'you', and so on. An example using the word 'record' might be 'Recall every copy representing David'. So long as the children have produced a recognizable message, they can all be winners, but you could award prizes for the funniest or most imaginative!

ONE TO TEN
Age 7–10

A memory word game for older children, this is best played by a small group, probably no more than eight, otherwise the first children in each round always have least to remember – and the last have an almost impossible task!

The children sit in a circle. The first child thinks of an object which begins with 'o', to go with 'one', such as 'one oyster'. The next child says 'One oyster and two tangerines'. The third child says 'One oyster, two tangerines and three televisions', and so on up to ten. Anyone who forgets one of the objects is out. You then go back to the beginning and add an adjective to the objects already mentioned, so that the second round might go 'One oily oyster', 'One oily oyster and two tasty tangerines', 'One oily oyster, two tasty tangerines and three tiny televisions', and so on round the circle up to 'Ten tall trees', or whatever. Once again any child who misses any part of the round is out. Keep on adding adjectives to each round until the final Mr or Miss Memory has been found.

If you find you have a group of super-brains, make the list go up to twenty or more!

THE PARSON'S CAT
Age 6 +

This is a simple alphabet game with no particular winners, but it does make the children think. It's also a good game for waiting times and journeys.

The children have to think of an adjective to describe the parson's cat in alphabetical order round the group. For example, 'The parson's cat is an angry cat'; 'The parson's cat is a beautiful cat'; 'The parson's cat is a crazy cat' and so on.

ON THE FARM
Age 3 – 6

A rowdy but sedentary game. With a younger group of children, it is probably best to have one or two adults sitting in to help give everyone the right idea, and make sure they understand what to do.

All the children sit on the floor in front of an adult, who is the storyteller. Give each child the role of a farm animal that makes a recognizable noise, such as a chicken, cow, sheep, goat (distinguish these by making one say 'maa' and the other 'baa'), horse, pig (a favourite), turkey ('gobble gobble' will do here), goose ('hissss'), duck, dog, cat – even mouse or rat ('squeak squeak'). If there are more children than animals then let them double up, this doesn't matter since the object of the game is to make as much noise as possible! The adult then begins to tell a simple story (write it out beforehand if you're not confident about ad-libbing), bringing in all the animals. Every time you mention the chicken, the child (or children) who is the chicken clucks loudly, similarly with the cow, pig, and so on. Also, every now and then, bring in the phrase 'And then they all woke up!', at which point all the children should make their animal noises at the same time as loudly as they possibly can.

You need to explain carefully beforehand what the children should do, and, especially if there are children who haven't played before, have a 'dry run' to make sure everyone is listening properly to the story and understands what's required of them.

WHIZZ BANG

Age 8 – 10

This is a game for sharp-witted mathematicians, which under-eights can play too if they're geniuses – and you'll soon find out once play is underway! As it's a completely cerebral game it's also a good one to while away the time on a journey to the pool or cinema, or waiting for the football game to start. (See pp. 116–19 for more ideas for games to play on journeys.)

Sit the children in a circle or line. Start numbering from 'one' on, with each person saying the numbers one after the other. However, at 'five' – or any multiple of five – the child whose turn it is says 'Whizz', and (much harder) at 'seven' – or any multiple of seven – the child whose turn it is says 'Bang'. Thus: '. . . twenty-four, whizz, twenty-six, twenty-seven, bang, twenty-nine, whizz, thirty-one . . .' and so on. Anyone who misses a whizz or a bang at their turn is out. Keep on numbering until you can't divide by seven in your head any more (calculators strictly not allowed!).

Pencil and paper games

WHAT'S ON THE TRAY?

Age 8 – 10

This is a memory game for older children. It is a good game for winter or wet day parties.

Before the party, assemble a collection of about twenty smallish and very different objects – some familiar and some not so familiar – on a tray and cover them with a cloth. A selection might include a box of matches, an apple, a squash ball, a comb, an egg cup, a key, a pencil, a pair of compasses, a credit card, a nail, a nail file, a penny, a walnut, and so on. Make sure everyone has a pencil and paper ready, but not in their hands when they view the objects on the tray. Place the tray on a table where everyone taking part has a good view. Give them exactly thirty seconds or one minute to look (depending on age and the number of things on the tray), then quickly cover and remove the tray (shapes under the cloth can be a giveaway if it's still in view). Give everyone exactly two minutes to write down as many of the objects as they can remember. You can give two prizes if you want – one to the person who remembers the most objects, and one to the person who has spelled most of them correctly!

FEEL IT

Age 8 - 10

This is similar to What's on the Tray? *except that it uses the sense for touch rather than sight. Depending on the number of guests, it takes quite a long time as each child has to do it separately.*

For this game, you need a large cardboard box with dividers, the sort that wine and spirits merchants use to pack bottles in is ideal. These dividers leave spaces that are just big enough for a child's hand and arm. At the bottom of each divider place an object to be felt; choose items of different sizes, textures and shapes, but obviously nothing sharp or dangerous. A selection might be a tangerine, a shoelace, a comb, a cotton-reel, a dog biscuit, a paper clip, a potato, and so on.

Blindfold each child in turn and let them feel inside each of the dividers to try and guess what each object is. Then give him or her a pencil and paper to write down as many as possible. When every child has felt inside the box, read out the actual contents so that the children can check whether they were right and how many they remembered. The child who remembers the most objects correctly wins.

SLIMY AND SOPHISTICATED FEEL IT

A popular variation of *Feel It* is to make all the objects disgusting to feel – the slimier the better. Peeled grapes, peeled, hard-boiled eggs, cold porridge, cold spaghetti, shaving foam or hair mousse, a wet soap bar, and a damp sponge or flannel all have the desired effect!

A more sophisticated version of this game is to guess objects by their smell. Lay out some very strong-smelling things in a shallow cardboard box (a tray is too shallow and the smells disperse too quickly). A selection could include garlic, cloves, a peeled banana, scented roses, washing powder (this has a very distinctive smell), coffee beans, mint, Plasticine, and so on. Once again, blindfold each child in turn and give them thirty seconds to have a good sniff into the box, without looking or touching, and then let them go away and write down any smells they recognize. This is a difficult game, but intriguing.

ANAGRAMS

Age 8 - 10

This is an absorbing game for bright eight- to ten-year-olds on their own; it's also fun for a mixed party of children and adults.

Give each player a piece of paper and a pencil and in a given amount of time – five minutes, say – get them to write down as many words of two or more letters as they can make out of one long word or combination of words, which they write at the top of their piece of paper for reference. The word could be an obvious long word like Parliament or Mathematics, or it could have a relevance to the party itself, such as the full name of the host, like Caroline Smith or Vijay Patel, or it could be the name of the celebration, like Birthday or Christmas.

CONSEQUENCES

Age 8 - 10

This is an old favourite which goes down well in a mixed children's and adults' party, such as at Christmas or New Year's Eve.

As with *Heads, Bodies and Legs* (see p. 63), supply everyone with a large piece of writing paper and a pencil or pen. The idea of this game is to build up a very strange story as the papers get passed round – the more people playing the better! First of all everyone writes a male name at the top of the paper, folds it over and passes it on to the next person, who writes 'met' and a female name, folds it over and passes it on. The next step is to say where they met – on, in, under, at, wherever. After this, the stages are what 'he said to her', then what 'she said to him', then 'the consequence was' – in other words, what happened. Finally, everyone writes what 'the world said', rather like a newspaper comment. Pass the papers round one more time and then everyone reads theirs out in turn, usually with great difficulty because of the amount of laughter!

Some children really enjoy the challenge of this game, so you can make it even more complicated by adding in adjectives as separate stages at the beginning, as in 'Hairy / Bugs Bunny / met unspeakable / Madonna'.

ALPHABET LISTS

Age 8 - 10

This game is another simple race against time. Your own child might like to help you choose suitable and appropriate categories for your guests.

Provide everyone with a paper and pencil and give them two minutes exactly to write down as many things from a particular category as they can, beginning with the same letter. The categories could be girls' names, towns, animals, pop stars, TV programmes, birds, flowers, dogs, and so on.

Indoor games and races

Team games are best played by children of school age; in a group of younger children – even up to five-year-olds – you may find some who are not mature enough to co-operate in team games and who are unable or unwilling to play games which require turn-taking. Even older children may be shy about joining in if they don't know many of the other children. If this is the case, make sure that you – not the children themselves – decide who is going to be in which team so you can at least try to make them evenly balanced.

There's no reason why inclement weather should stop you organizing races – you just have to be more selective about the ones you choose to do if you are going to be indoors!

Team games

BALLOON VOLLEYBALL

Age 5+

This is an active game which has to be played indoors – a balloon is too light for outdoor play, the wind will blow it away.

Divide the children into two evenly matched (or equally dissimilar!) teams. Rig up a simple volleyball net – a piece of string hung at a suitable height (just above the tallest child's head) will do. A paper chain or streamer is more decorative, though it's more liable to break during play. The object of the game is simply to bat the balloon over the 'net' for as long as possible. Every time one team drops the balloon or lets it fall to the floor, or knocks down or breaks the net (which happens quite often!), the other team scores a point. Bursting the balloon scores a penalty to the other side – five points and they have to blow up the next balloon! Play for five minutes then change sides.

BEAN BAG QUOITS

Age 5-8

Another good indoor game, this could equally well be played outside. Vary the distance between the throwing line and the box according to the children's ages – the older they are, the further they should be able to throw.

Borrow some bean bags from your local school or gym, or make your own by filling squares of tough cloth with dried pulses. You'll need one for each child taking part. You'll also need two deep cardboard boxes. Mark out a throwing line with tape or chalk in a suitable room and set up the two boxes far enough away from the line to give all the children a reasonable chance of throwing a bean bag into the box.

Divide the children into two teams. Each child in turn has to throw his or her bag into the box – the team to get the most bean bags into the box wins.

BALLOON BETWEEN THE LEGS

Age 4+

This is a team game for a group of children. For the younger age groups (four- and five-year-olds) don't have more than four in the teams. Have more than two teams or race in heats instead.

You need two large balloons – the bigger they are the more awkward the game! (And have some in reserve in case of bursts.) Divide the children into two or more teams and stand them in lines, one behind the other. The first person in each team holds the balloon between his or her ankles. When you say 'Go', or blow a whistle, each team has to pass the balloon backwards between their legs, without using their hands and without stepping out of line. If the balloon goes out of the line, if anyone touches it with their hands or if it bursts, the team has to start again from the beginning, in the last case with a new balloon.

CHIN TO CHIN
Age 7 - 10

Everyone finds this team race difficult, but seven- to ten-year-olds will enjoy the challenge. So that it's fair, make sure the teams are either all roughly the same height, or all equally asymmetrical!

Divide the children into teams of four or five, no more, and stand each team in a line shoulder to shoulder. Give the first person in each team a large orange which they have to hold under their chins. When you say 'Go', or blow a whistle, the teams have to pass the orange from one member to the next, chin to chin, without using hands. Anyone who drops the orange can use his or her hands only to position the orange under their own chin again.

CAT LAP
Age 7 - 10

This can be a simple race between a few children, or arranged as a team relay, depending on the number of children at the party. It's best reserved for the older age group – younger children might choke in their hurry.

Provide saucers of milk, fruit juice, squash or whatever drink is most popular. Make sure that all the saucers have exactly the same amount in them. Put the saucers on the floor (protect your carpet if necessary from spills) and make the children kneel on all fours like cats. When you say 'Go', or blow a whistle, they have to lap up the liquid like a cat – the first to leave a clean saucer wins!

BALLOON CHIN TO CHIN

Although younger children won't be able to play *Chin to Chin* as well as the older age group, they may like to try to play it with a small balloon, passing that from one chin to the next in teams. Don't be too strict about hands for the under-sevens, and if you think you have a child who won't be able to cope with a burst balloon, it's best avoided.

FOOT RACE
Age 7+

An indoor team race for the nimble-footed!

Divide the guests into two equal teams and sit them on chairs in two rows opposite one another, with their feet together and their legs stretched out in front of them. The idea is to pass a tennis ball (or any other ball of similar size) along the row, only using the feet! The ball can be retrieved by hand if it falls but it must be passed on to the next person using only feet.

LIFE-SIZE NOUGHTS AND CROSSES
Age 8+

This is a fairly quiet but absorbing game.

Mark out a giant noughts and crosses square with tape or chalk. One team becomes noughts and the other crosses – give them large cards to hold to make it easier. Choose one or two members of each team to decide the positions (change this each round to avoid argument), then play in the usual way, with the children acting as the noughts and crosses standing in place. Score two points for a win, one for a draw and nil for losing – the first team to reach ten points wins.

LIFE-SIZE DRAUGHTS

This is a variation on *Noughts and Crosses* for a really large party of older children (they must understand how to play the real game well). Mark out the board as for *Noughts and Crosses,* and colour the squares with either pieces of card or old carpet tiles.

This could equally well be played outside.

ON THE LAP
Age 6+

This exciting relay race can be played indoors or out. If you have a mixed age group, make sure you line up the teams so that the heaviest and strongest children go first.

Prepare two identical, simple obstacle courses side by side, according to the available space and equipment (see pp.100–1 for ideas). Divide the children into teams of four or five and line up each team behind a sturdy upright chair. When you say 'Go', the first child in each team has to run round the obstacle course and come back and sit on the chair. When the next child has completed the obstacle course he or she has to sit on the lap of the child sitting on the chair, and so on until all the children in the team are sitting on each other's laps. The winning team is the one with all its members on the chair, with their feet off the ground.

STEPPING STONES

Age 6-10

This is quite an active, noisy team game but it can be played very successfully indoors, which makes it useful for winter parties. The stepping stones could simply be cut from sheets of paper, but this does tear rather easily so card, offcuts of carpet or, if you can get them, carpet tiles are more satisfactory.

Scatter 'stepping stones' over the floor between two marked points at either end of a fairly long room. The stepping stones should be big enough to accommodate the average foot size of the children attending the party, but not much bigger, and far enough apart for the children to reach with a big stride. Divide the children into two teams. The first team lines up at the start while the other team assembles on either side of the course (make sure they don't stray on to the course itself). When you say 'Go', the children in the first team have to cross the room on the stepping stones only, while the opposing team does everything possible, without actually touching them, to put them off so that they lose their balance. Any child who touches the floor instead of the stepping stones has to go back to the beginning and start again. Give each team two or three minutes (carefully timed) during which as many children as possible try to complete the course and cross the finishing line. When the time's up, the teams change places. The winning team is the one that manages to get most children over the finishing line in the allotted time.

ROLLER BLOW

Age 6-10

This is a similar team game to Water Slalom *(see p.79), except that it's played on dry land (probably the carpet!). You need to collect the cardboard holders for toilet paper and kitchen paper towels for this game.*

Cut up the cardboard centres of toilet rolls or kitchen paper towels into 70mm (2½in.) lengths. Create two or three twisty obstacle courses, depending on the number of children and therefore teams you have, with books, wooden blocks, plastic beakers or any similar objects. Give each child in the team a piece of cardboard roll and a good strong straw. When you say 'Go', the first child in each team has to blow his or her roll round the obstacles. (Make sure that everyone understands which way round they have to go.) As soon as the first child has finished, the second in each team starts. The first team to blow their rolls round the course wins.

If you want to make this game more complicated, devise a course which involves going right round some of the obstacles (without bumping into them and knocking them over), or even doing a figure of eight.

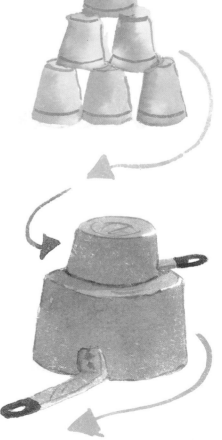

TWISTERS

Age 7-10

This game is marketed commercially but there is no need to buy the mat; it is fairly easy to make one yourself. Agile children will enjoy this – and they'll particularly appreciate a few unselfconscious adults having a go too.

You'll need a piece of stiff cloth or polythene about 1.5m (4ft 6in.) square. Using paint or indelible markers fill in twelve large circles – big enough for a child's foot to stand on – in different colours. Space the circles out reasonably well. Divide the children into two teams. The second child in each team instructs the first child in the opposing team, telling them to place their feet and hands on particular colour circles. Child A from Team 1 calls to Child B from Team 2, for example, 'Put your right hand on pink.' Then Child A from Team 2 might call to Child B from Team 1, 'Put your left foot on green.' So far so good. It becomes difficult when the children are then instructed to put their other hand on purple or their other foot on blue, especially if these are either behind them or on the other side of the square! The idea is to try to make the child on the mat twist so much that he or she loses balance. Once the child falls over, he or she is out and the next member of the team takes his or her place. The team with a child still standing (or balancing) when all the members of the other team have overbalanced wins.

BLOW FOOTBALL

Age 7-10

Endlessly fascinating, this game requires only simple equipment, but you will need a couple of linesmen and a sharp-eyed referee whose decision everyone must agree is final.

You'll need straight straws (not the type with a bend near the top), a table-tennis ball and a large, straight-sided tray. Bind opposite ends of the tray with a different colour and divide the children into two teams, assigning a colour to each team. In heats of two a side, the children have to blow the table-tennis ball from their end and try to score by hitting the other end of the tray. At the same time, they have to prevent the opposing team blowing the ball against their own end. Allow two-minute periods and keep a running total – the team with the most goals wins.

WATER SLALOM

Age 5+

This game is slightly less frenetic than Blow Football *but requires quite a lot of concentration.*

You'll need two deep rectangular roasting pans or washing-up bowls. Fix a line of four or five straight straws upright in the bottom with Plasticine or Blu-tack. Then fill the bowls about half-full with water. Divide the children into two teams and provide each child with a straw. They race against each other in twos. Carefully float a table-tennis ball at the nearest end of each bowl. When you say 'Go', or blow a whistle, the children have to blow the balls in and out of the upright straws like a slalom — first one to the other end of the bowl wins, and the next child in the team has a go. Award five points for a win and take away two penalty points for a slalom post being knocked down. The team with the most points at the end wins. (This is a fairer way of calculating than a simple 'winner takes all' as it means that the team that wins has probably been the most careful.)

Games for groups

BARMY BOWLING

Age 4+

This is an excellent game, especially if you have a long straight corridor in your home — if you live in a block of flats, ask the neighbours and the caretaker if they have any objections to you playing in the communal passageway.

You don't need to have professional-looking skittles for your party version of bowling — in fact, the whackier the better. Use anything unbreakable that will stand upright. Liquid detergent bottles, plastic squash bottles, wellington boots, toddlers' stacking toys stacked up, and cardboard tubes from the middle of kitchen paper rolls, are all suitable. You'll also need a reasonably heavy ball, like a softball, cricket ball, a boule or croquet ball, to roll.

Set up your skittles at the end of a corridor with a pile of cushions behind them so that the ball doesn't damage the wall or the person restacking the skittles after each hit. Mark a bowling line a suitable distance away. Give each skittle a score from one to six — mark it on the skittle in some way as visibly as possible (stickers are probably easiest). Then as each child takes turns to bowl, add up his or her total score from the numbers of the skittles actually knocked down. If they down all the skittles with one ball, add twenty to the score. Allow three turns each so each child can improve his or her aiming skills each time.

BALLOON BATTING
Age up to 5

This is what the under-fives can play instead of Balloon Volleyball, inside or out!

There aren't really any rules to this game – just provide as many balloons as you can blow up and get the children to bat them with their hands into the air for as long as possible. Expect some to burst, and therefore some children to be frightened. If this happens, make sure there is a quiet place for them to go and play away from the balloon game.

WHAT'S THE TIME, MR WOLF?
Age 4-7

This exciting game could equally well be played outside.

Start by having an adult play Mr Wolf, after the first game the more confident children will want to take on the role themselves. Choose an area to be 'home' – it's got to be big enough to accommodate almost all the children playing the game, so the wall of a room or a large sofa might be suitable. Mr Wolf prowls around the house with his back to the children, who all follow him at a safe distance, but not too far away! The children chorus 'What's the time, Mr Wolf?' at regular intervals, at which point Mr Wolf turns round, and everyone stops as he says 'One o'clock' or 'Eleven o'clock' or 'Twenty past eight' or whatever. But at some unspecified point, he answers 'It's dinner time!' and all the children have to run as quickly as possible for home as Mr Wolf chases after them to try and catch as many as possible. The first child to be caught becomes the next Mr Wolf.

ELIMINATION MR WOLF

In order to avoid argument, and to make *What's the Time, Mr Wolf?* more competitive you could play it without changing the person who is Mr Wolf. Instead, all the children who Mr Wolf manages to catch are out, and you go on playing the game until all but one child has been caught. (The fewer children there are, the harder it gets to escape Mr Wolf.) The last child is the winner (it's frequently more than one child in fact).

WHO, WHAT, WHERE, WHEN

Age 6+

A good game for an active group of children, this could also be played outside. If you do play out of doors, designate strategically placed objects for each command, for instance, a tree for 'Who', a garden chair for 'What', and the shed or a door for 'Where'. Obviously, they just sit on the grass as fast as they can for 'When'.

Group the children around you and designate one side of the room as 'Who', one side as 'What' and another as 'Where'. 'When' is the floor. As you shout out the four words completely randomly they have to rush over and touch the correct side of the room, and when you say 'When' they have to sit on the floor. Anyone who gets it wrong is out – and the last one in wins.

O'GRADY SAYS

Age 5+

This indoor game allows one of the children to be bossy, without being told off!

Choose a child to be O'Grady. (With a younger group who haven't played before, it's a good idea to start off with an adult in this role.) O'Grady stands in front of the other children and orders them to do things: for example, 'O'Grady says do a somersault'; 'O'Grady says sing "Baa Baa Black Sheep"'; 'O'Grady says clap your hands three times', and so on. As long as the command begins with 'O'Grady says', they must do it; however, if O'Grady orders them to do something without prefixing it with 'O'Grady says' (for example, just 'Turn round three times'), then they mustn't do it. Anyone who does is out.

GRANDMOTHER'S FOOTSTEPS

Age 5-7

This traditional game manages to combine quietness with activity – a good mix!

Choose a 'Grandmother' from among the guests, or let an adult take the first turn to make sure everyone understands the game in the first round. The Grandmother stands face to a wall with her hands over her eyes. All the other children stand behind a marked base line. While the Grandmother faces the wall, the children creep up from the base line towards her. But when the Grandmother turns round (she can do this at any point), all the children have to freeze, standing as still as possible. Anyone seen to be moving by the Grandmother has to go back to the base line and start again. The Grandmother turns her back on the children again and they creep forward again, and she turns and tries to catch them moving again. The child who manages to reach the Grandmother and touch her back first takes the next turn as Grandmother and the game begins again.

HIDE AND SEEK
Age 6 +

Although better for the over-sixes, this perennial favourite is enjoyable for younger children if the range of hiding places is limited and adults are on hand to help the seeker in case of problems. Hide and Seek *can be played outside as well as in, especially in its more active form as* Forty-Nine Relieve-O *(see p. 102).*

Choose a child to be the seeker, and station him or her at a place designated 'home' – a free-standing sofa is good as it is difficult to defend on all sides. The seeker covers his or her eyes and counts to 100 while everyone else goes and hides. When the seeker reaches 100, he or she shouts a warning, usually 'Coming, ready or not', and then starts to look for the hiders. They have to try to reach 'home' before being caught – anyone who reaches home without being caught is safe – and the first person to be caught is the seeker next time.

SARDINES
Age 6 +

A traditional game – but none the worse for that – this is usually acceptable to older children as an alternative to Hide and Seek. *You need to be able to allow as much of the house as possible to be used for this game, so make sure that out-of-bounds areas are clearly indicated and that there's nothing that could fall and hurt someone hiding.*

Choose one child to go and hide, while everyone else counts up to 100 together. The children then go their separate ways to find the hiding child. If anyone finds him or her, instead of making it known they squeeze into the hiding place as well. Gradually other children will probably find the hiding place too, and as many children as possible squeeze (like sardines) into the hiding place until there isn't room for anyone else and the hiding place becomes obvious to everyone! The first person to find the hiding child hides next time.

PASS THE PARCEL

Age up to 7

This game has practically become a standard item, like the birthday cake, at young children's parties, and with a little help it's perfectly acceptable for toddlers' too. It is perennially popular right up to six or seven, and is a good game for calming down after something rowdy like Stuck in the Mud *(see p. 103), or after the party tea.*

Starting with a small gift in the middle, make up a large parcel with layers of old paper, using enough layers to give every child at the party at least one turn at unwrapping. So many people interleave the layers with a sweet or small gift that after a couple of parties most children come to expect this. A single jelly or perhaps a piece of chocolate money is all that is necessary, and if you don't want to single out any one child to 'win', make the gift in the middle of the parcel exactly the same as the items you are interleaving. Use any waste paper for the parcel layers; tissue paper is very good for younger children as it is easy to tear away. Newspaper is obviously an option, although the ink does come off on hands and clothes so avoid it if you don't want to have a long hand-washing session, or if you don't want to send children home with soiled clothes. Fix each layer with a single piece of thin sticky tape – any more will be frustrating.

Sit the children in a tight circle. Choose a suitable tape with continuous music, as for *Musical Chairs* (see p. 45). The children pass the parcel from one to the other around the circle and when the music stops the child who has the parcel takes off a layer of paper, and so on until the whole parcel has been opened. Keep an eye on the parcel so that every child gets a turn at unwrapping. If you have made a few more layers than children, you can make the last few turns completely random, which is of course how the game was originally played!

If you are playing with an older age group of six- and seven-year-olds, make it entirely random by making sure that the person controlling the music cannot see where the parcel is going.

SLEEPING LIONS

Age 4 - 8

This is a very good game for indoor parties – you know where everyone is, you don't need music or words and it doesn't involve any running about! As such, it's perfect after a hectic game of Hide and Seek *or* Musical Bumps. *You could probably make this last for three or four rounds as children think they get better at it as they go on – in fact, after a couple of rounds, they are usually laughing so much that they get worse!*

If there are a lot of children, choose two children to be 'It' (if there are eight children or less, pick out one child only). All the other children become sleeping lions, lying flat on their backs on the floor as still as possible, and with completely straight faces. The 'Its' go round and try to make the sleeping lions laugh. They can do anything they like – such as pulling funny faces – but without actually touching them. Anyone who laughs is out – the last one or two lions in at the end take over as 'It' in the next round.

APPLE ON A STRING

Age 4+

This is very similar to Apple Bobbing *(see p. 100) except that no-one gets wet and it is probably easier to play indoors. It is almost as difficult as apple bobbing, but younger children do enjoy having a go. In their case don't make it a race, just a fun activity.*

Skewer several apples and run a string through each of them, securing the string with a large knot. Hang the apples at a suitable height for the children to try and catch them in their mouths. The children either stand or sit with their hands behind their backs and try to take bites out of the apples. This is quite a difficult game so don't be too rigid about the rules – the best thing is to allow a time limit, and let the children have the apples to eat afterwards anyway.

FORFEITS

Forfeits is an interesting variation on *Everybody Out.* Instead of eliminating the children and making them leave the dance floor, you could make them do a forfeit, for instance, 'Everyone whose name begins with B has to drink a glass of water backwards' or 'Everyone who had chips yesterday has to sing "I'm Dreaming of a White Christmas".'

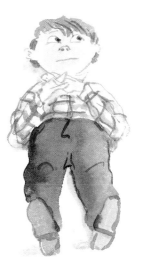

EVERYBODY OUT

All ages

Although children of all ages can play this game, it is a particularly good one to play at a pre-teen disco – the DJ can call the forfeits.

Get the children to dance in the usual way but every now and then stop the music and call out something which could eliminate some of the children from the dance floor. For example, 'Everybody out . . . who's wearing something pink.' Then later, 'Everybody out . . . whose name begins with B.' Next, 'Everybody out who had chips yesterday', and so on. Make sure you've got a good list of eliminators and think about them in relation to your guest list so that there's little chance of anyone slipping through the net eventually.

RING AROUND THE RING

Age 5-8

This is another sitting-down game which still manages to be exciting.

Thread a ring on to a piece of string long enough to go round all the children sitting in a circle. Choose one child to sit in the middle. The children in the circle hold the string with their hands curled over it, fingers forwards so that it's difficult to see where the ring is. They then pass the ring round the circle as quickly as possible while the child in the middle has to guess where it is. The children are allowed to try and confuse the guesser by pretending to pass it along even when they haven't got it. The child who is passing the ring when the guesser gets it right becomes the next guesser.

SILLY SQUASH

Age 7-10

This is a very active game which has to be played indoors, and is particularly good for winter parties with a group of excitable children, as a way for them to let off steam.

You need a three-sided space big enough for two children to swing a bat, but it doesn't have to be a regular shape. A garage, a wide hallway, a room, a large shed or barn would all do. Clear away most of the furniture and anything precious on the walls. You also need a beach tennis set – plastic racquets and a light foam ball (you can often buy these in garage forecourt shops, toy shops, resort shops and even supermarkets during holiday periods). You could also use table tennis bats, but don't use a ping-pong ball as it would be too rigid. The foam ball won't do any damage in itself – it's too light and squashy – but it is important to remove all breakables as the ball or the children could easily knock something over.

Depending on your wall surface, tape or chalk a play line round three sides of the 'squash court' at a suitable height (test this out with your own child beforehand). To play, two players at a time (as in real squash) bat the ball anywhere above the line, allowing play from volleys or from one bounce only. The idea is to keep the ball in play as long as possible; the first child to miss or allow two bounces is out. Play the game as a simple knock-out, with the winner of each game taking on the next player – the last one still in when everyone else has been eliminated is the overall winner.

TOURNAMENT SQUASH

For a large party (eight or more) of active children, play *Silly Squash* as a proper tournament. Work out a full play list, as for a tennis tournament. Pair off the children, and let them play the first round. The winners of those rounds (depending on how many children you have) then play quarter- and semi-finals. Finish with a grand final.

HUNT THE THIMBLE

Age 5 - 7

For this traditional game, the children have to be quite sharp-eyed and need to be able to stop themselves from blurting out the position of the thimble. For this reason, it is worth having a dry run if there are any children present who have never played the game before.

Keep the children out of the room while an adult places a thimble somewhere visible but unobtrusive. Don't put it too high – bear in mind the average height of your guests. (If you haven't got a thimble some other small object would do, but either way make sure that you have shown it to the children so that they know what they are looking for.) Then, let the children into the room to hunt for the thimble. They mustn't touch anything, they must just look. When they have located it, they mustn't say anything but simply sit down with crossed legs to indicate that they know where it is. The last person to sit down is out and the first person to sit down hides the thimble next time – but to avoid cheating make the child show you where the thimble is once everyone else has located it and is sitting down.

Indoor races

TORTOISE RACE
Age 5+

This game is deceptively difficult – the back of a child on all fours is by no means flat and the pillows slip off remarkably easily once the children have started to crawl.

Provide all the children with a pillow – if you haven't got enough to go round (or don't have enough space to let all the children race at the same time), organize the race in heats of four at a time. Line the children up on all fours, resting on their knees and elbows, rather than their hands, with the pillows lengthways down their backs. Mark out a suitable course (over a carpeted floor preferably) and get the children to race across it. If the pillow falls off they have to go back to the beginning, so they can't go too fast.

FILL THE POT
Age 6+

This race requires patience and skill and very gentle movement from the children. You could equally play it as a team relay game.

Give each child a straw. Place a saucer containing ten or twelve small sweets such as chocolate drops, dolly mixtures or Smarties for each child on a table at one end of the room. Put a yogurt pot per child on a table a metre or two away. When you say 'Go', the children have to suck up the sweets one by one at the end of the straw and drop them into the yogurt pot on the other table. Any sweets dropped *en route* have to be put back into the saucer and sucked up again. Obviously the first person to have all the sweets in their yogurt pot wins – but you may as well let them all eat their sweets as well!

DRESSING UP RACE
Age 4+

All children love this game. Younger children may have more difficulty dressing themselves but you could have a version for them involving only one garment each.

Provide a set of very large old clothes for each child. Again, if you haven't got enough to go round, organize heats of four at a time. Provide trousers or a skirt (trousers for girls, skirts for boys might be novel), a large shirt, a jacket or sweater, a scarf, a hat and a large pair of shoes or boots. Place the clothes in piles at one end of a large room, and mark a finishing line at the other end. When you say 'Go', the children have to dress themselves so that they are wearing all the clothes and then jump or hop, rather than run, to the finishing line. If any item of clothing comes off or falls down, they have to go back to the beginning and put it back on before restarting.

BACKWARDS WALKING RACE
Age 5-7

This race will probably appeal to under-fives as well as the five-to-seven age group – at least it will give any spectating adults a lot of laughs!

Very simply, mark out a race course in a large room. Line the children up with their backs to the winning post and make them walk backwards to the finishing line. No running, no turning round and undoubtedly lots of falling over!

THE CHOCOLATE CHOP

Age 7-10

A hilarious game for a large group of children, this can become quite frenzied, so expect deafening noise and occasional squabbles as the children change places.

The children sit in a large circle either on chairs or on the floor. Place three normal-sized bars of chocolate on three plates, each with a knife and fork, on a table 2–3m (6–8ft) away. Put a chair by each plate and place a pile of silly clothes – such as an old shirt, a scarf, a hat, a pair of gloves and a pair of enormous socks – on each of the chairs. Each chair should have the same number of items of clothing and they need to be easy to put on and equally easy to take off.

Distribute three dice round the group, equal distances apart. The children who have the dice throw them. If they don't throw a six, they pass the dice quickly clockwise on to the next child, who also throws as quickly as possible, and so on round the group. If any of the children throws a six, he or she has to dash over to the table, put on all the silly clothes, and then try to cut a piece of chocolate with the knife and fork. If they succeed in cutting a piece, they can of course eat it. The catch is, however, that they have to do all these actions before another child has thrown a six, because as soon as this happens, the new child has to put on the clothes and start cutting up the chocolate. This is fine while only the first three children to throw sixes are at it, but once more children are involved they have to take the clothes off the children at the table and put them on themselves.

There are no real winners in this game – the children enjoy just racing against time and the fall of the dice. You can, however, stop the game if everyone is getting overheated and, of course, if they succeed in demolishing the chocolate.

DICEY DOINGS
Age 7-10

You can make this game as difficult or as easy as you like, depending on the skill and dexterity of the children at the party.

Sit the children in a circle as for *The Chocolate Chop*. On a nearby table, set up six rather tricky things to do, like threading a darning needle with wool, peeling a tangerine, doing up a shoelace or shoe buckle, sticking drawing pins in a potato, doing up a divided zipper such as on an anorak, or sharpening a pencil. None of these should be at all difficult for a normal seven- to ten-year-old, except when they are wearing an outsize pair of gloves, which you also need to supply – one pair per task! Designate each task a number from one to six. The first child throws the dice. If, for example, he or she throws a three, he or she must run up to the table, put on the pair of gloves next to the task marked '3' and try to do it before another child throws a three. The same thing happens for a child throwing a four, six or any other number. If another child throws a particular number before the first child to have that number has completed his or her allotted task, the second child has to take over, putting on the gloves and trying to do the task. The first person to finish the task before the number is thrown again wins. (As with *The Chocolate Chop*, this doesn't often happen in practice!)

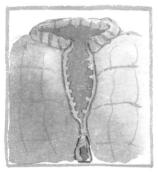

Blindfold games

Some of the pencil and paper games on pp. 64–71 require blindfolds, but only to sharpen the wits of the children playing. These games depend on blindfolds for their *raison d'être*. Younger children are sometimes frightened by blindfolds if they have never played a game involving one before – if any child starts to panic, quickly remove the blindfold and let another child try instead. Use a soft scarf made of silk or a similar material in a dark colour so that it will stay on without being tied too tightly; woolly scarves slip off. Better still, see if you can get hold of an airline face mask, the sort of thing they give you on long-haul flights when you want to sleep.

Single blindfolds

TAIL ON THE DONKEY

Age 3-7

This is a traditional favourite.

Draw or paint the donkey – without its tail – on a large piece of paper and tape or Blu-tack it to the wall at the right height for the children to reach easily. (It might be dangerous if they have to climb on to a chair when blindfolded – even with supervision, children can become disorientated and may fall off.) It is best to make enough tails for everyone to have his or her own, each with the child's name written on it, and use Blu-tack or double-sided sticky tape, rather than pins, for fixing. Alternatively you can mark the place with a cross and write in the child's name. Stand each child in turn in front of the picture so they can have a good look at it, then blindfold the child, making sure he or she has the tail ready. Turn the child round three times before letting him or her try to stick the tail in place. The child whose tail is nearest the donkey's rump wins.

DIFFERENT DONKEYS

It needn't, of course, be a donkey. If you want to vary *Tail on the Donkey*, try putting the tail on the elephant, the nose on the clown, the astronaut in the rocket, the wand in the fairy's hand, and so on. It all depends on your child's taste and your own talent as an artist!

BLIND MAN'S BUFF

Age 4 -7

This is another old favourite, but it is not worth playing if the children do not all know each other very well beforehand. It is best played in a fairly confined space so that the child who is blindfolded has a better chance of catching one of the others.

Choose one of the children to be the 'blind man', and blindfold him or her. Everyone else dodges out of the way if possible while the blindfolded child gropes around trying to catch one of them. Once he or she does succeed in catching one of the children, everyone has to keep very quiet while the blindfolded child tries to guess from the feel of the captured child who it is. If he or she guesses right, the captured child becomes the next 'blind man'.

BLINDFOLD PORTRAITS

Age 4 -7

This is another hilarious game, but of course no-one wins. It's probably best played by a smallish group of children – if they have to wait too long for their turn, some children will get bored and disinterested.

Set up an easel with lots of large pieces of paper, or tape or Blu-tack sheets of paper on to a wall one after the other. Blindfold each child in turn and get them to draw a simple object – a horse, an elephant, their mum, a tree, a house. As an added hazard when they have finished, get them to write their names on the bottom of the picture as well! Give them their efforts to take home at the end of the party.

SQUEAK, PIGGY, SQUEAK
Age 4-8

Like Blind Man's Buff, *this game should only be played if all the children know each other very well. Younger children enjoy it for its own sake, so there is no need for prizes: they often cannot resist giggling, so give themselves away anyway! Older children can win points for guessing correctly or for foiling the blindfolded child by skilful squeaking.*

All the children sit in a circle on low chairs. (The height is important as the blindfolded child has to be able to sit on another child's lap with ease.) Choose one of the children to be blindfolded. Stand the child in the middle of the circle of seated children, and twist him or her round three times. Everyone has to keep very quiet so that there are no audible clues as to which child is which. The blindfolded child then gropes towards the edge of the circle until he or she finds one of the seated children, and sits on the child's knee. The blindfolded child then says, 'Squeak, piggy, squeak', whereupon the seated child squeaks in as strange a way as possible. The blindfolded child then has to guess who is making the noise. The 'piggy' takes the next turn with the blindfold.

Pairs and groups

PRISON BREAK-OUT
Age 7-10

This is a blindfold game for older children. You need several referees or linesmen for fair play.

Divide the children into two teams. Mark out a large room or the garden into three distinct areas with lines of string – prison, the prison yard, the outside world. One team are prisoners, the other prison guards. Blindfold the prison guards and get them to sit spread out over the area designated as the prison yard. The prisoners assemble in the prison, and when you give the command (clap your hands or blow a whistle), they begin to creep across the prison yard to safety. The guards have to try to hear the prisoners passing and if they do they point straight at the prisoner. The referee blows his or her whistle (or claps hands) and everyone else stays still. If the guard is pointing correctly at a prisoner then that prisoner has to go back to prison till the end of that round. Allow about three minutes per round, then change over so that guards become prisoners. The team with the largest number of escaped prisoners in the outside world wins.

ARE YOU THERE, MORIARTY?

Age 7+

This is a very silly game which is as amusing to watch as it is to play.

Make big hats out of folded newspaper – you could get the children to make their own beforehand. Blindfold two players at a time and get them to sit in front of each other on the floor, each armed with a rolled newspaper sword, which is long enough for them to be able to reach the other's hat. The first player calls out: 'Are you there, Moriarty?' and his or her opponent has to answer 'Yes!'. They then have to try and knock each other's hats off with their rolled-up newspapers. The first person to lose his or her hat is out and the next challenger takes his or her place. Continue the game until there is an overall winner.

FEED THE BABY

Age 5+

This silly game is one way to use up uneaten party food. If you use sloppy food like jelly, make sure the 'babies' are all wearing bibs, and cover the floor with newspaper or plastic sheeting if you're worried about spills.

Divide the children into pairs, or play the game one pair at a time – like *Are You There, Moriarty?*, it's an excellent spectator sport as well as fun to play. Blindfold the pairs, and tie tea-towels round their necks to protect their clothes. Each pair sits on chairs opposite each other, knee to knee. Provide each child with a bowl of food – jelly, ice-cream, mousse or similar – and a spoon. They have to try to feed each other with the contents of their bowls. There are no winners in this game – just a mess!

Outdoor games and races

Once your children reach the age of six, races are always popular, though obviously you need space to run them, and to play games of tag, successfully. If you don't think your own garden is adequate, take them all out to the nearest park or recreation ground. You'll need at least one other adult to help – more if you are taking them out, simply to make sure none of them wander off. A word of warning: don't make race tracks too long for relays or events with heats, or those waiting their turn will get bored. It's worth finding out what is reasonable with a couple of children of the right age and size beforehand.

Outdoor races

PANCAKE RACE
Age 7+

You can't expect the children to toss pancakes from a frying pan – this is a good variation.

Cut out pancake shapes from stiff paper or thin card and lay them on two sticks about 60cm (24in.) long; the children hold one stick in each hand. They then have to run over a marked race course without letting the pancakes drop.

HOPPING RACE
Age 5+

Hopping is a skill which isn't usually mastered much before the age of five, and for five- to six-year-olds don't make the course too long.

This is sufficiently difficult for all ages that you can happily let a mixed age group race off against each other. Disqualify anyone who runs and anyone over seven who changes legs in the middle!

SOMERSAULT RACE

Age 4+

This is a good game for indoors as well as out. Like hopping, somersaults are difficult for the under-fives and few children of that age can do them more than once without help.

Again, this is something that all the children can race against each other. Disqualify anyone who takes any steps at all between somersaults, but don't be too hard on the ones who aren't quite as gymnastically perfect as the others. For this race it is especially important not to have too long a course – work out what is reasonable beforehand.

WHEELBARROW RACE

Age 5 +

Allow a lot of space for this game to avoid collisions – it's best played outside.

This is a pairs race – pair off the children yourself rather than letting them do it. You need a smaller, lighter child to be the wheelbarrow. The child who is wheelbarrow walks on his or her hands, while the other child holds up the wheelbarrow's legs. Advise them to tuck the legs under their arms, and support the calves with their hands, and make sure that they don't push the wheelbarrow children too hard or their arms will give way.

RELAY RACES

An interesting variation on simple races, like hopping or somersaulting, is to run relay races. Divide the children into teams, and get them to hop out and somersault back. Once the first child is back, the next one in the team starts hopping. Don't make the baton they have to hand on too big or pointed – for younger children, it's probably better to use a piece of cloth or ribbon or a band that the children actually have to put on over their heads. Obviously, the first team to complete a hopping leg and a somersaulting leg for each child wins.

WHEELBARROW SLALOM

A variation on a simple wheelbarrow race, a wheelbarrow slalom is a good idea if you find your pairs are too speedy at the ordinary race. This is probably best organized in heats. Set up two or three lanes, each containing bean poles or some other obstacle that the wheelbarrows have to weave in and out of.

If you do run the race in heats and are going to expect the winners to race off against each other in a grand final, it's particularly important that you don't make the course too long.

SACK RACE
Age 7+

It's quite difficult to get hold of old-fashioned hessian sacks nowadays, and ordinary black plastic rubbish sacks won't last – at least not more than one race, anyway. The best thing to do is to go to a builder's merchants and buy heavy-duty plastic sacks (the sort that they use to take away rubble).

Race the children against each other or in heats, depending on the number of sacks you've got. (If you've got strong sacks, they should withstand several heats of jumping!) This race is probably best for the over-sevens as the children have to be tall enough to hold their sacks up – they won't be able to do it if they are swamped by the sack. The children take their shoes off, and stand by their sacks. When you give the signal, they climb into their sacks and jump to the finishing line.

THREE-LEGGED RACE
Age 4+

Even quite young children enjoy attempting this race. Like the Wheelbarrow Race, *it needs lots of room, so play outside.*

Pair the children off yourself by height, although for an amusing diversion for older children you could make the pairs as disparate as possible! Tie their inside legs together (not too tightly) at the ankle with long scarves or neck ties – anything else will be uncomfortable and for younger children could be dangerous. If they haven't done it before, advise them to put their arms round each other's shoulders or waists. Let all the pairs have a practice run around to start with. This is a race best run in heats as there is always lots of weaving about and (especially) falling over.

FOUR-LEGGED RACE

As a variation on a three-legged race, or for a large, older age group, try a four-legged race – that is, with three children tied together. This is quite hard, especially on the middle child who has both legs tied and therefore cannot keep his or her own balance but has to rely entirely on the other two children!

BICYCLE SLALOM

Age 7+

This again is probably best in the park, and for kids who like to show off their BMX skills (although conventional bikes are just as manoeuvrable).

Mark out three or four lanes with garden canes or bean poles. The canes should be spaced 2–3m (6–10ft) apart and, for safety, they should be more than 2m (6ft) tall – higher than the cyclists in case they fall against them. This is a speed race so the poles are bound to be knocked over – make sure there are plenty of adults ready to set the fallen ones upright again immediately, and one to add up the penalty points. Have no more than four lanes with four poles in each so that everyone stands a chance of gaining points – and losing them if they touch the poles. Award points for winning: twenty for first place, say, fifteen for second, ten for third, and five for fourth, and have a penalty of three points lost for every pole touched. Run several heats and then if the scores at the end are close, have a sudden-death ride-off without points – the winner is the one who gets there first!

EGG AND SPOON RACE

Age 6 +

This is an old favourite, but none the worse for that.

Hard-boil the eggs beforehand for your own peace of mind, and also to avoid accidents – a slimy broken egg on the race track could cause quite a nasty slip. The simple version is to place the eggs on dessert spoons and let the children run over a marked race course.

A variation is to make the children run with an empty spoon to a tray at the other end, where they then have to pick up an egg and run back with it. Turn this into a relay race by making each team pass on the spoon and pick up an egg in turn.

SLOW BICYCLE RACE

Age 7+

Unless you've got a really big garden, you need to go to the park for this.

Make sure the guests have been told to bring bikes, alternatively, run the race in heats if you've got three or four bikes you can supply yourself. Obviously, this is a race for accomplished bike riders. The idea of a slow bicycle race is to come last – the last one over the line without putting a foot on the ground or falling off is the winner!

OBSTACLE RACE
All ages

You don't necessarily have to hold obstacle races out of doors, although obviously you can cover a lot more ground and be more adventurous if you do. You can also make an obstacle race do for almost any age range so long as you are sensible about what the children are capable of. If you are going to set up an obstacle race for fives or under, make sure nothing that requires climbing is higher than about 60cm (24in.) as children lose their balance very easily if they are over-excited and distracted. Also, make sure there are lots of other adults on hand – and don't make it too competitive for little ones. For the older age groups – six and over – make it a race against time (you'll need a stop-watch or something similar), and have a chalkboard to update individual times, say on a best of three basis, depending on the number of children taking part. For young children try to have an adult stationed by each obstacle to help – one to two is probably enough for older children, especially to make sure they don't take short cuts! You can use almost anything you like as an obstacle, although you may have to use a good deal of ingenuity to get hold of suitable equipment.

A typical outdoor course for the over-sixes might consist of jumping in and out of a propped-up tyre; crawling under a net; running along a specified course with an egg in a spoon (hard-boil it – see *Egg and Spoon Race*); crossing stepping stones (it's safer to use old cushions or pieces of carpet tile rather than anything higher off the ground); slaloming between garden canes, old fence posts, even chairs, either crawling or hopping; running on tin-can stilts; sucking up six Smarties or similar small sweets with a straw and placing them in a bowl (also with the straw); wellie-wanging (throwing a rubber boot as far as possible or over a specified marker); and somersaulting over the finishing line.

An indoor obstacle race for under-sixes might consist of jumping in and out of one or more hoops laid on the floor; bouncing six times on a toddlers' trampoline (if you haven't got one or don't know anyone who has, you might be able to hire one from a local gym or playgroup where they are pretty standard equipment); crawling through a tunnel (play tunnels are also readily available, but you can make a perfectly acceptable one with a low coffee table and a blanket); balancing on a bench (not too high); hopping round a sofa; putting on some big item of clothing that gets in the way (like an old shirt); and skipping or jumping to the finishing line.

Games of tag

FORTY-NINE RELIEVE-O

Age 7+

A sophisticated version of Hide and Seek, *this requires a large and preferably quite wild or wooded area for best effect, although a large garden or shrubby park is suitable. It's an ideal game for a summer picnic party, but does need adults to be on hand – preferably playing as well – to make sure no-one gets lost. You need a base or 'home', as the idea of the game is to reach it without being caught and the child who is 'it' has to defend the base. In other games of tag being 'it' is usually quite popular. In* Forty-Nine Relieve-O, *however, being 'it' is often not so popular as you are a bit isolated and with a skilled group may well find yourself being 'it' again!*

Choose one child to be 'it'; everyone else goes off to hide. The child who is 'it' stays at the base and counts to forty-nine, then calls 'Coming ready or not!' He or she then starts to look for the other children. As 'it' has to defend the base, however, the child who is wise does not stray far away from it. Meanwhile, the children who have been hiding gradually work their way towards the base, using whatever cover there is available. If the child who is 'it' spots one of the hiding children, then he or she shouts the name and 'I've seen you', and if correct, the named child has to make a dash for base, hoping that he or she can get there without being caught. If caught, the child has to wait at base to be freed, if not caught then the child is safe and will not have to be 'it' next time. If a child is caught, he or she can call 'Forty-nine relieve-o' to let other children know that he or she needs to be freed. This happens when a child gets through to base without being caught often, in fact, without even being seen which can happen when 'it' is absorbed in chasing someone else. The child who gets through without being caught can then free anyone else who is imprisoned at the base.

The end of the game comes when all children have reached base – with or without being caught. If all the children are free when this happens then the same child has to be 'it' again, otherwise the first child to be caught and not freed by someone else becomes 'it'. If you think a child who has to be 'it' twice running is going to be upset or really can't cope, intervene and choose someone else (use one of the methods outlined on pp. 42–3).

FRENCH TAG

Age 6 +

Simple games of tag like French Tag are always popular and children can sustain them for a long time without getting bored. As with the other games of tag, this requires someone to be 'tag' or 'it' or 'he' – there are so many different terms for this role – so it's best to be ready with a suitable method of random choice (see pp. 42–3). This is probably the simplest of all the tag games, but you do need lots of space to play successfully.

Choose one person to be 'tag'. He or she then runs about trying to catch someone. Once a child is caught, he or she becomes tag and the original tag is free. The secret of this fast-moving game is to keep tabs on who is tag at any particular moment.

STUCK IN THE MUD

Age 4 +

It's worth scheduling this energetic game towards the end of the party, when it doesn't matter about clothes getting dirty, as the children have to crawl between each other's legs.

Choose a person to be 'it'. He or she rushes around trying to catch as many children as possible. When a child is caught, he or she has to stand still with legs apart until released by one of the other children who has to crawl between the legs of the child 'stuck in the mud'. To allow several children to have a turn at being 'it', time each child's turn and then blow a whistle and choose the next child to be 'it'. Three- or four-minute bursts are quite enough for this energetic and hilarious game.

CHAIN HE
Age 6+

Another hilarious game. As with the other tag games, there are no winners or losers – they go on until everyone drops from exhaustion!

Choose one child to be 'he' as usual. He or she rushes around trying to catch as many children as possible. The snag is that when a child is caught he or she has to hold hands with the one who is 'he' and form a chain, which gradually gets longer and longer and more and more unwieldy. As with *Stuck in the Mud*, it's best to have timed turns so that more than one person has a chance to be 'he'.

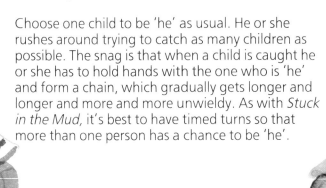

Other outdoor games

THE FROZEN SPOON
Age 8–10

This is a team game for lively older children to play out of doors on a hot day. It involves much screaming and hilarity, especially if it follows a really energetic game like French Tag (see p. 103).

Place two ordinary metal dessert spoons (not from your best cutlery set) in the fridge at least three hours before the party.

Just before you play the game, tie the end of each spoon to a long length of strong twine – smooth parcel string is better than the rougher sort of garden or packing twine. You will probably need a full, unused ball for each spoon if there are more than about four children in each team. The two teams stand side by side in a line. You then pass the frozen spoon to the first child who has to thread it up one sleeve, across his or her back and out of the other sleeve. (If anyone is wearing a sleeveless dress or T-shirt, lend them an old shirt or something with sleeves.) They have to pass the spoon as quickly as possible to the next person who threads it through in the same way until you have a whole group of children strung together. The team which is threaded together first wins.

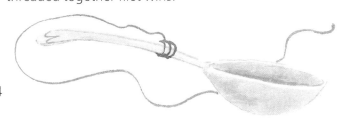

APPLE BOBBING
Age 7-10

Definitely an outdoor game for warm days – it is almost impossible to stop children getting very wet in this game, which is always enthusiastically received. Children much younger than seven simply won't be able to do it, and the five- and six-year-olds may well not have enough teeth to do the job properly, even if they want to!

Divide the children into two or three – or even four, if there are a lot of them – teams. Provide a washing-up bowl of water for each team, with lots of apples floating in them. (Don't use buckets –

they are too deep.) It is a good idea to use knobbly cooking apples or windfalls with their stalks intact, since these are much easier to bob than smooth round eating apples from the supermarket shelf, even though they may not be very nice to eat raw! Provide more apples than there are children in the team as they may need more than one try. Seat the children on the ground in lines a little way from the bowls, with a clean, empty bowl beside each team. When you say 'Go', or blow a whistle, the first child in each team runs up and kneels over the bowl, and tries to lift an apple out with his or her teeth – no hands allowed! They then run with the apple in their teeth and put it in the clean bowl, at which the next child runs up and bobs the next apple. The first team to bob an apple for each child wins.

Ball games

JUMPING JACKS

Age 6 - 10

This is an active outdoor game for a large group of older children. You need plenty of space, so it's a good one for a picnic party in the park.

Divide the children into two teams, with badges, sashes or some other sort of marker to distinguish them. Mark out two large squares about 5m (15ft) apart and station the two teams within them. Then provide one team with several large balls, which are not too hard as they could hurt. When you blow the whistle, the team with the balls have five minutes to roll them at the team on the other side and try to hit them below the knee. They must only throw from inside their marked square. The children in the other team have to jump to avoid the balls, which they are not allowed to touch or kick, and they must also stay inside their marked territory. If any of the children are hit by a ball they have to go over to the other side, and if any child goes out of his or her territory or interferes with the ball, he or she also has to change sides. After five minutes, blow a whistle and count the number of children who have been captured by the first team. Then give the balls to the other side and give them five minutes to see how many children they can capture. The team with most captives wins.

DOUBLE JACKS

A variation on *Jumping Jacks* for the eight-to-tens is to provide both teams with balls so that they are bombarding each other, and also to let the captured children try and escape back over the no-man's-land to their own territory. The opposing team can try to hit them with balls if they see them doing this. This version of the game can be quite rough and needs a lot of supervision.

106

FRENCH CRICKET

Age 5+

This is a good game even for quite small gardens, since it doesn't involve running about. Use a tennis racket and a soft foam ball – the beach tennis kits used for Silly Squash *(see p. 86) are ideal.*

Choose a child to bat first. He or she holds the racket down at foot level and is not allowed to move from the spot, only to turn the racket round. All the other children take turns to throw the ball and try and get the batsman out by hitting him or her on the leg below the knee. The batsman in turn tries to avoid this by protecting his or her legs with the racket and hitting the ball as far as possible, scoring runs by passing the racket round and round his or her body. The batsman is also out if someone catches the ball. The person who gets the batsman out is the next batsman in.

WHO'S GOT THE BALL?

Age 6-8

A good ball game for a smallish group who know each other quite well, this could also be played indoors if you have a reasonable amount of space and a soft foam ball.

Choose one child to be 'It'. He or she takes the ball and stands with his or her back to the other children, who stand in a group about 2–3m (10ft) away. The child with the ball throws the ball backwards over his or her shoulder to the other children, who have to be very quiet. One of them catches it (or picks it up from the floor) and holds the ball behind his or her back. All the other children pretend to be holding the ball behind their backs as well, and then all shout 'Who's got the ball?' At this, the child who is 'It' turns round and has to try and guess which of the children really is holding the ball. If he or she guesses right then the child who is holding the ball becomes 'It', if wrong he or she has to try and guess again.

BEAT THE BALL

Age 3-6

Even the under-fives (although not the under-threes) get great satisfaction out of this outdoor game because they are racing a ball rather than each other. Younger children will enjoy the game for its own sake (so there is no need for prizes), but you could award prizes to five- and six-year-olds who beat the ball.

Line up the children on either side of you. Roll a large, fairly heavy ball which will roll well (a football is ideal) along the ground to a designated spot at the other end of the garden. As soon as the ball leaves your hands (but not before – watch for false starts!), the children start to run and try to get to the other end of the garden before the ball does. Anyone who interferes with the ball – and this is usually done by accident! – is out.

Acting games

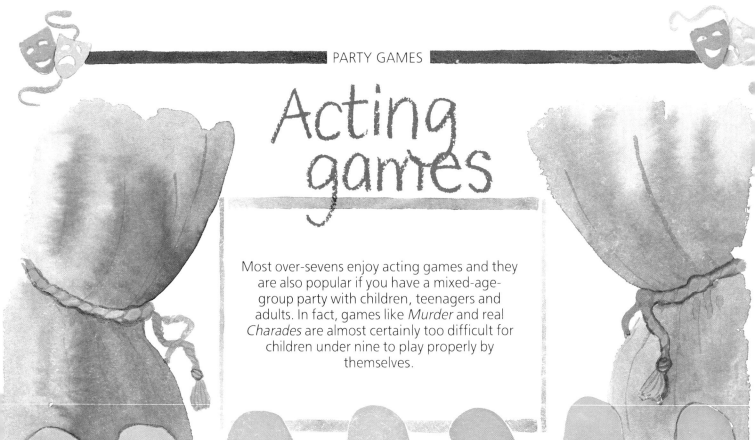

Most over-sevens enjoy acting games and they are also popular if you have a mixed-age-group party with children, teenagers and adults. In fact, games like *Murder* and real *Charades* are almost certainly too difficult for children under nine to play properly by themselves.

Miming games

IN THE MANNER OF THE WORD

Age 8 - 10

This is quite an educational game as well as being fun since all the members of the miming team must understand the meaning of the word chosen in order to act it out. Have an adult on hand to help them make their choice and advise on miming it while they are out of the room.

Divide the guests into two teams. One team goes out and chooses an adverb among themselves. When they come back into the room, one after the other, they must mime various commands from the opposing team 'in the manner of the word'. The opposing team has to guess what the word is – when they get it right the teams change places and the game begins again. For example, the first team might choose the adverb 'timidly'. The opposing team might then ask the first child to brush his or her hair 'in the manner of the word'; they might ask the next child to jump up and down, or make tea and so on. Each time the child in question has to try and act it out 'timidly' until the opposing team guesses the adverb. If they can't guess it by the time every child has had a chance to try acting it out, then the first team has another go.

108

DUMB CRAMBO

Age 8 - 10

This game, which is also commonly known as The Game, *was popularized in the UK in a television version between celebrity teams.*

Divide the guests into two teams. Give each member of the team the title of a well-known book, play, television programme, film or pop song on a piece of paper. The team members then have to act out the title in a complete dumb show, and the opposing team has to guess the title. There are various clues which can be used to help. To start with, the mimer can indicate what kind of title it is by a selection of signs – opening hands like pages for a book, winding a hand projector for a film, making a square with hands for a TV programme, indicating opening curtains for a play, turning a finger round and round like a needle going round a record for a song title. The mimer indicates the number of words in the title by the number of fingers he or she puts up, and then which word he or she is going to act out, also by the number of fingers. Little words, like 'the', 'a', 'of' and so on, are indicated by putting the thumb and forefinger close together. If the mimer wants to act out the whole title at once, he or she can indicate this by sweeping the hands round to indicate the whole thing. Members of the opposing team can ask questions but the mimer can only nod or shake the head in response.

For example, if the title is *The Phantom of the Opera*, the mimer would indicate that it is a play by raising the curtain. He or she should indicate that there are five words and that the first word is small. Putting up two fingers indicates that he or she is going to act out the second word, then he or she could pretend to be a ghost. For the last word (indicated five), he or she could pretend to be an opera singer. By this time, the other team will almost certainly have guessed the title. One of their team then has a turn, and so on.

109

WHAT'S MY LINE?

Age 7-10

Based on one of the earliest TV panel games, this is a useful standby for winter parties with a mixed group of over-sevens.

Write down a number of simple actions on slips of paper and place them in a box. Some examples are 'chopping wood', 'milking a cow by hand', 'knitting a sock', 'lighting a fire', 'grilling sausages', and so on. One by one children pick out a slip of paper and act out the task. The rest of the children then have to try and guess what was being done by asking questions which can only be answered by 'Yes' or 'No'. Give them a time limit of three or four minutes (or a limit of twenty questions, depending on how hard the tasks are to act out), otherwise the game will go on too long and not everyone will have a turn at acting.

Word games

MURDER

Age 9-10

This is an exciting, and exacting game, for older children, which has to be played after dark, hence its other title Murder in the Dark.

Place as many pieces of folded paper as there are guests in a box or bag. All the papers should be left blank except for two – one says 'Detective', the other 'Murderer'. The detective declares him- or herself and sits down well out of the way of the other guests, but everyone else keeps quiet. Then, put all the lights out. Everyone moves around the house as much as possible, but without touching one another. This is important because the murderer has to 'murder' his or her victim by tapping him or her sharply three times on the shoulder. At this point the victim shouts 'Murder!'

as loudly as possible and stays exactly where he or she is, and the adult in charge of the lights turns them all on as quickly as possible. The murderer has to try to get as far away from the victim as possible in the short time available. As soon as the lights go on, everyone assembles where the detective has been sitting and he or she asks everyone questions about where they were, what they were doing, and so on. Everyone has to be absolutely truthful, except the murderer who can tell lies, but people can give each other alibis if they know they are true. (The victim, of course, doesn't enter into the proceedings at all.) Allow a time limit or a limited number of questions for the detective to single out the murderer – when he does so he says, 'I accuse you of the murder.' If he is right then the murderer must own up and becomes the detective next time, when only a murderer is selected from the box or bag. If the murder is unsolved, choose both a new murderer and detective.

CHARADES
Age 8-10

There seem to be many versions of this game, but this is a favourite, and an excellent one to play at big mixed-age-group parties.

Divide the guests into two teams. One team goes out into another room and chooses a word, usually quite a complicated word with more than two syllables, although if you are playing with a group of children on their own, a two-syllable word might be better. Choose some suitable words beforehand and be ready with notes on suggested scenarios to save time.

The children have to work out little plays to act out the parts of the word, with some dialogue which includes something that sounds like the part of the word, and ending with a tableau to include the whole word. For instance, if the word was 'Comfort', the two first scenes could include the words 'Come' and 'Fort', while the last would include 'comfort'. The children will probably need quite a lot of assistance; in this example you could suggest that two of the children were mothers with younger children meeting in the street, with dialogue that ran:

'Hallo, Mrs Green, how are you today?'

'Well, I'm fine, Mrs Smith. Would you like to come and have a cup of tea?'

'Yes thank you, I don't mind if I do.'

The idea is that there should be plenty of short words in the conversation to put the opposing team off the scent, but without letting the scenes get too complicated. The second scene in this example could be the US cavalry riding up to relieve a fort, with dialogue running something like:

'Look, General Custer, there's the fort, it looks like we've managed to get there just in time!'

Finally, there should be a simple scene involving the whole word, such as a child falling down in the playground at school and hurting him- or herself. One of the other children could pretend to be the teacher, saying perhaps:

'Oh dear, little Johnny has fallen and hurt himself. You go and fetch the first aid kit, while I go and comfort him.'

Treasure hunts and guessing games

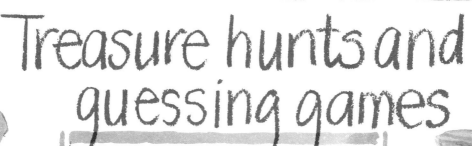

Treasure hunts with clues are complicated to organize but rewarding as older children generally find them absorbing. However, don't make them too difficult, or those who aren't so keen will soon give up and may become disruptive or cheat. Also, don't let them cover too wide an area or you may lose track of where all the children are. There are alternatives to clues, so choose a version to suit your group. Make sure you label areas which are out of bounds.

Games for individuals

FOLLOW THE TRAIL

Age 6+

This is a good game for a party of relatively few older children (six is probably the optimum number), which can be played indoors or out. As it takes a while to set up and can't work if it's broken or destroyed, it's best played as the first game of the party.

Have a ball of wool or string for each child and fix the ends to one particular place, such as a mantelpiece or newel post. Attach a notice with each child's name on each yarn trail. Then run the yarn all over the house or garden in as intricate a way as possible, ending up in a particular place where a 'treasure' can be hidden. It doesn't matter if the different strands overlap and intermingle, this just makes the game more interesting! To start the trail, make sure each child has the end of his or her strand; then all they have to do is follow their trail wherever it leads, rolling up the string or wool as they go.

X MARKS THE SPOT
Age 6+

Older children may like to help prepare this game.

On a large piece of paper draw a map of an imaginary island (in the rather graphic illustrated style of old-fashioned maps, if you can). Give it as many features as possible – mountains, caves, bays, rocks, inlets, coral reefs, palm trees, native settlements, rivers, lakes, jungle, and so on. You could even give it forts, castles, dungeons – the possibilities are endless and your helpers are bound to have good ideas too. Somewhere on the island is hidden treasure. Before the party, mark the place on the back of the map with a pin hole or another almost invisible marking. The children have to guess where the treasure is buried by marking the map with a black cross; write their names beside each cross. Then later on, perhaps just before going home time (the suspense makes this game more exciting), look at the back of the map and see whose cross is closest to the buried treasure – whoever's cross is nearest wins.

FLAGS IN THE SAND
Age 6+

This is a similar treasure hunt game to X Marks the Spot, *and equally exciting.*

Fill a shallow box – such as a seedling tray or plant box – about half-full with dampish sand, so that a cocktail stick will stand up in it. Draw the area of the sand tray on to a large piece of paper, such as newspaper, and decide where the treasure is going to be buried, then hide your template! (Older children may like to decorate the sand tray to make it look like a desert island, with rocks, palm trees, jungle animals, and so on.) Make flags by sticking small pieces of stiff paper to cocktail sticks, and write each child's name on to a flag. Ask each child carefully to stick his or her flag into the sand at the point where they think the treasure is buried. After a suitable interval of suspense, get out your paper template and place it over the box to see which flag is closest to the point you chose for the buried treasure. The child whose flag is closest to the buried treasure wins.

HUNT THE SWEETS
Age up to 5

There's no need to exclude the youngest children from treasure hunts with this simple game.

For younger children, simply hide sweets in obvious places for them to find, in one room or part of the garden to avoid disappointment.

From about the age of four, you could hide small presents labelled with each child's name. This might be a good way to end a party, with the gift as an alternative to a party bag.

For pairs and threesomes

TREASURE HUNT
Age 7-10

The classic treasure hunt for older children is time-consuming to organize since it involves clues dotted about which lead on to the next clue and so on, eventually ending up with the treasure. They are, however, universally popular.

Divide the children into pairs or threesomes (make sure there is enough treasure for all at the end) and give them the first clue before they set off. Clues can be anagrams (for example, 'Vot then' – 'on the TV'), crossword-type clues (perhaps, 'Underneath what Polly put on' – 'Under the kettle'), or relatively simple (for example, 'In the cupboard', but without specifying which one). Choose ones suitable for the age of the children playing. Clues must not be removed, and no-one from any team should tell another team what they mean. The first pair or team to find the treasure wins.

INDIVIDUAL TREASURE HUNT

If you don't want to make this a competitive race, just a fun activity, you could give each team its own set of clues. That way, nobody will be stepping on anyone else's toes, and everyone will end up with some treasure that they've found by their own efforts. However, you will have to be quite creative to come up with more than a couple of trails this way!

PAIRS
All ages

This is a useful starter game – the versions get more sophisticated the older the children are.

Pre-school version: Cut up large pictures into two asymmetrical halves. Old greetings cards or large postcards are excellent for this. (Never throw these away, keep them somewhere in a box for just such an occasion – at other times your children will enjoy cutting them up to make collages.) If you use magazine pictures, you should stick them on to stiff paper before cutting them up. Distribute one half of each picture around the party room in reachable positions. These should be very obvious for the twos and threes but can be a bit more subtly placed, without actually being hidden, for the fours and fives. Give each child the other half of one of the pictures and set them all off at the same time to find their matching half. (You could write their names on the back as an additional clue.) The first child to find it and lay out the two halves the right way up to make the complete picture wins.

Five-to-seven version: *Pairs* is a good game to pair off older children into couples, for instance for *Silly Squash* or a *Three-Legged Race* (see pp. 86 and 98). As each child comes in, pin one half of a picture on the back of their clothes. Hand half of another picture to them to look at. Each child has to find the half that matches the one in their hand on the back of another child. The first two children to be paired up win, or take first turn at the next paired-off game.

Over-seven version: This is basically the same as the previous version, except the cards have one half of a famous pair written on. Keep these fairly obvious, such as 'Laurel' on one, and 'Hardy' on the other. If you don't want to use famous duos, choose other pairings like 'Peaches' and 'Cream', 'Bangers' and 'Mash' or 'Socks' and 'Shoes'. Alternatively, you could have a baby animal theme such as 'Cat' and 'Kitten', 'Dog' and 'Puppy', 'Horse' and 'Foal', 'Hare' and 'Leverett', 'Bird' and 'Fledgling', 'Frog' and 'Tadpole'.

Games to play on journeys

Many parents like to dispense with conventional party-giving after their children reach the age of about seven, preferring to take a small group on an outing to a play, sports event, circus, cinema or even to a restaurant for a special meal (see p.35 for ideas and advice). You may think that party games aren't necessary if you decide on this course of action, but in fact if your chosen treat involves more than about twenty minutes' journey time, you will need to have some absorbing games to keep the children occupied, especially on the way there when they are very excited. For obvious reasons, these games are not suitable for the under-fives.

Recognition games

LICENCE-PLATE ALPHABET

Age 5+

This is a good game for a car journey of half an hour or more. Remember to exclude those letters which aren't used – I, O, Q and Z in the UK.

As you drive along, the children look out for licence plates which include first the letter A, then B, and so on through the alphabet. Make sure that at least one other child has seen the plate in question; if no-one else can confirm the sighting, you have to look for that letter again.

I-SPY
Age 5+

This traditional favourite is good for a mixed-age group, because the objects spied can be as obvious or obscure as the child choosing can manage. In fact children look at the world in such unusual ways that sometimes adults in particular are very surprised by the things they choose in this game!

Choose a child to take the first turn (or let an adult do it to make sure everyone understands the game). He or she looks around for a suitable object, either inside the vehicle or out, but it must be visible to all the children, and then says, 'I spy with my little eye, something beginning with . . .', and gives the initial letter of the object. If the object, for instance, is a church on the horizon, the child would say, '. . .something beginning with "C".' If the object is outside the vehicle in which you are travelling, make it clear to the child that the object must be visible for the whole time the other children are trying to guess – so it is no good spying a tractor in a field if you have passed it three miles back! (If you are travelling at speed in, say, a train or tube, confine the objects to be spied to the interior of the carriage.) Everyone then looks round for objects beginning with the letter in question, and each child calls out his or her guess. The child who guesses the object correctly takes the next turn. If the object is so obscure that no-one manages to guess in a given time limit (say three minutes), the child gets another turn.

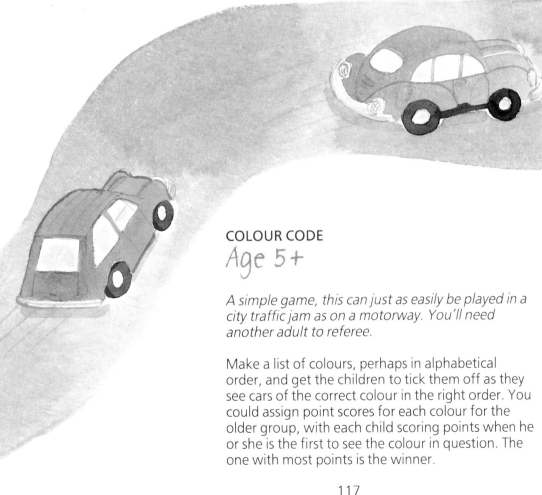

COLOUR CODE
Age 5+

A simple game, this can just as easily be played in a city traffic jam as on a motorway. You'll need another adult to referee.

Make a list of colours, perhaps in alphabetical order, and get the children to tick them off as they see cars of the correct colour in the right order. You could assign point scores for each colour for the older group, with each child scoring points when he or she is the first to see the colour in question. The one with most points is the winner.

PLACE-NAME ALPHABET
Age 6+

Once again, this helps to while away the time on longish car or bus journeys. If you are travelling through a city, you could use street names instead.

For a journey of less than thirty minutes, the children look out for place or street names containing first an A, then B, then C and so on through the alphabet. (On motorways, get them to read the exit signs.) For really long journeys, look out for place or street names actually beginning with the letters of the alphabet in order.

ROUTE-MAP ALPHABET

For a train or tube journey, where it may be difficult to make out the names of the stations, get the children to play *Place-Name Alphabet* by reading the route map. (Many stations will provide a route map with a timetable if you don't think they are posted in the carriages.) You can also play the game this way on a car journey using a road atlas. Pass the atlas round the children in turn and get them each to find a place name beginning with the letters of the alphabet in correct order, using only those pages of the atlas which include the journey you are actually taking.

Estimating games

MILE-A-MINUTE
Age 7-10

This game is for long journeys on motorways which have emergency telephones placed at equal distances along the side of the road. It is only possible to play this game if the motorway is reasonably clear and you can travel at a regular speed – not one for heavy traffic or contraflow systems! In addition, this is a game which requires a non-driving adult to referee; it would be dangerous for a lone driver to try to run this game.

Point out to the children the emergency telephones by the hard shoulder along the route. Work out roughly how far apart they are in terms of time, by counting slowly but steadily from one to sixty or thereabouts (this is probably the correct count if you are travelling at between sixty and seventy miles per hour). In the UK, emergency telephones are usually placed about one mile apart, others may be one kilometre apart – you can probably check this on the milometer or distance counter on your dashboard. Once the children have established the counting speed, wait for the next telephone to come into view. As you pass it, say 'Now!' The children then have to drop their heads and hide their eyes until they think they have reached the next telephone. When each child thinks you have reached it, they call 'Now!' without opening their eyes. As you drive past the emergency telephone, the referee says 'Here!' and everyone opens their eyes. The child who called out 'Now!' nearest to the telephone wins. They can usually guess the distance quite accurately by counting up to sixty at the required speed, but as they are having to do it in their heads it requires a lot of concentration and practice. It is surprising how the miles can fly by when children are absorbed in this game.

SO NEAR, SO FAR
Age 7-10

This is similar to, but less complicated than, Mile-a-Minute, *and can be played on any type of road. It too needs the help of another adult apart from the driver.*

The group chooses a distant object, but one which you are obviously going to pass quite close to the road. It could be a tall tree, a church, a cottage, an inn or roadside restaurant, a filling station, factory or office block, or even a prominent advertisement hoarding. Make sure everyone knows exactly what they're looking at. The children then have to guess how far away it is in miles, kilometres or fractions of these. The driver checks the distance on the milometer or distance counter – all modern cars have a trip meter which means that you can count exactly. The child with the nearest guess wins.

Index